T0099555

Ellen Braae

Urban Planning

in the Nordic World

Aarhus University Press / The University of Wisconsin Press

The Nordic World
Urban Planning in the Nordic World
© Ellen Braae 2022

Cover, layout, and typesetting:
Camilla Jørgensen, Trefold
Cover photograph: Ulrik Jantzen
Copy editors: Heidi Flegal and Mia Gaudern
Acquisitions editors: Amber Rose Cederström
and Karina Bell Ottosen
This book is typeset in FS Ostro and printed
on Munken Lynx 130 g
Printed by Narayana Press, Denmark
Printed in Denmark 2022

ISBN 978 87 7219 724 1
ISBN 978 0 299 33894 7

This book is available in a digital edition

Library of Congress Cataloging-in-Publication
data is available

Published with the generous support of the
Aarhus University Research Foundation,
the Carlsberg Foundation and the Nordic
Council of Ministers

The Nordic World series is copublished by
Aarhus University Press and the University
of Wisconsin Press

All rights reserved. Except for the quotation
of short passages for the purpose of criticism
and review, no part of this publication may
be reproduced, stored in a retrieval system,
or transmitted, in any form or by any means,
without the prior permission of the publishers

Aarhus University Press
aarhusuniversitypress.dk

The University of Wisconsin Press
uwpress.wisc.edu

PEER
REVIEWED

MIX
Paper
FSC FSC® C010651

Contents

Chapter 1.
Introduction

Spatial planning is never neutral. Nor is it exclusive to modern times, although it gained importance in the twentieth century and has since become closely linked to the production and distribution of public welfare. "Spatial welfare planning" is an attempt to manage a development in a community or society – either positively, steering it in a specific direction guided by a set of values, or negatively, with the goal of avoiding adverse trends or effects. The kind of urban planning that grew out of early industrialization processes aimed to mitigate the worst consequences of living next to the new industrial production facilities. Yet throughout history, the broader aims of ensuring access to water, food supplies, and good infrastructure, protecting inhabitants from risks, and optimizing local climate conditions have been integrated aspects of all human settlements. Urban spatial welfare planning aims to manage this metabolism and ensure control over the areas needed, as well as their use and development. This very frequently includes planning *for* and working *with* open spaces, and doing so across several scales – from the larger territory containing the main urbanized area(s), down to specific urbanization principles and relationships between built-up and open spaces. While these overall societal planning goals remain fundamental and thus relatively stable, the principles that guide planning and the prevailing understanding of what planning *is* have changed over time. As we will see, planning goals have also changed considerably over time.

Spatial planning is closely related to improving living conditions for citizens by means of a legal, economic, and cultural framework. Urban planning understood as spatial planning for welfare is an ongoing phenomenon that emerged in the United States and Europe after World War II (1939-1945); this book presents and discusses the topic in the context of the post-war era. While Britain played a key role, so did the Nordic world, and the focus here is on examples from Denmark, Sweden, and Norway, which served as prominent test beds for spatial planning to promote welfare. Yet, as we will see, spatial planning ideals and practices vary greatly among the Nordic countries.

Naturally, there is no simple response to the question of what characterizes Nordic spatial welfare planning. This book nonetheless offers some answers by giving an overview of the part of Nordic planning history that brackets the emergence of the welfare city. It demonstrates how, even while meeting new challenges, today's planning upholds and further develops that welfare legacy, in terms of hardware and, partly, software: the constructed traces, and the managerial structures. While managerial structures have changed significantly over time, buildings and landscapes physically embody various ideas of welfare, some of which have changed over time. These are the buildings and landscapes that we still inhabit, and that will continue to provide the material foundations for tomorrow's sustainable city - which must be constructed from today's imperfect city. The open spaces planned into our cities can be regarded as our green heritage, a legacy from the heyday of the welfare state, but they also represent both a challenge and the potential to help us address the crises of today and sustain the dreams of tomorrow. This book therefore focuses on the role of open spaces as a key and constitutive aspect of spatial urban planning, understood as embedded in a time–space continuum linking past, present, and future. Moreover, at its core is the issue of embedded welfare, its spatial materialization, and its use and reuse.

Back in the 1960s, the American architectural historian Kidder Smith boldly stated that Europe had given the world "the welfare city". Today this term is widely used to designate the huge processes of urban development that took place across Europe during the post-war decades, based on the belief that it was possible to literally build a better world. Fueled by the American Marshall Aid program, the aspiration of the European rebuilding process was twofold. The first aim was to avoid the failures of the period after World War I: the missed opportunities after the war ended in 1918; the Great Depression that had followed the Wall Street Crash in 1929; and the unemployment, inequality, injustice, and inefficiency resulting from laissez-faire capitalism, the indifference of an arrogant ruling elite, and the incompetence of an inadequate political class (Judt 2005: 67). Meanwhile, it was also clear that while the future would arrive one way or another, creating a *good* future would require planning. The second aim was, therefore, to pursue something more: better health, education, and transportation; more leisure opportunities; and decent housing for all. These aims presupposed a politically stable Europe. Another less pronounced aspect was that the Marshall Aid program would enlarge the American domestic market by turning Europeans into consumers of American products. In socio-economic terms, the result of the re-industrialization process was "a larger cake", which could be distributed to the population in the form of more, and more diverse, welfare services – creating a cycle of welfare production and welfare consumption.

Planning came to play a prominent role in the realization or "materialization" of European national welfare politics (Swenarton et al. 2014). Especially in the Nordic countries, planning became a central administrative instrument at almost all levels, from national to regional and urban, and, in principle, all the way down to the level of single buildings and local open spaces (Albertsen & Diken 2013). Just as there were many differences among other European post-war welfare nations, welfare policies, and welfare cities, there were also many differences among the Nordic countries and their welfare planning practices. Nonetheless, Denmark, Sweden, and Norway all built on the same social-democratic welfare model, as described by the Danish social scientist Gösta Esping-Andersen (1990). In his welfare model theory, the state, the market, and civil society are positioned to mutually interact with each other in various ways, and it is this overall mutual positioning that defines each welfare state model. In the Nordic model, the state plays the leading role and takes responsibility for the welfare of all citizens and residents, from cradle to grave and on a universal basis. This means that the state provides immaterial welfare services, such as education, healthcare, and daycare for small children and the elderly, as well as the material and spatial framework in which these activities unfold, such as recreational spaces, schools, hospitals, and town halls. Directly or indirectly it also provides a substantial amount of housing, albeit managed through a very decentralized system. The state is present at many levels of life in the welfare society: in regional bodies and counties, in municipal and local governments, on local boards of various kinds, and in contact with all the non-public entities such as sports clubs and cultural associations that receive public funding for activities that serve their local community or the population at large.

Urban planning and some basic points

One determining factor in the creation of Nordic welfare states that was present well before World War II was a long-standing democratic tradition. With Norway installing democratic governance in 1814, Denmark adopting a constitution in 1849 and Sweden doing so in 1917 – and with women in the Nordic countries gaining the right to vote at national elections in 1913 in Norway, 1915 in Denmark, and 1921 in Sweden – the democratization process was partly founded in the social reform movements that occurred in the latter half of the nineteenth century. In Sweden these were grounded in trade unions and several independent religious groups. In Norway they grew from strong social rights and women's rights groups, while in Denmark the agricultural cooperative movement was crucial in forming the Danes' self-perception. Danish political culture is partly the result of a specifically Danish modernization process that built on the learned experience that when people of humble means stand together, they can bring about significant change (Nielsen 2009). This basic experience can be traced from smallholders, the adult education movement, and the cooperative movement, via the trade unions, to various social and cultural movements in the twentieth century. These collective approaches brought new opportunities, but they also required negotiation and compromise with the already established society. For example, trade unions had to accept the employers' right to direct and distribute work. The democratic culture is reflected at multiple levels, and citizens generally participate a good deal in such activities. In this sense, the "citizen" element of Esping-Andersen's state–market–citizen triad cannot be regarded merely as a passive consumer. Another way of interpreting this highly democratic

11

culture is that "the Nordic welfare states combine the most decentralized governance systems in the advanced industrialized world with the most universalistic and egalitarian welfare system," resting on governance relations that build on a pragmatic consensus culture (Engberg 2017: 143).

Social reformist movements – which aimed to improve living conditions for ordinary people – had mobilized all over northern Europe during the nineteenth century in the wake of industrialization and urbanization, and they had instituted planning as a way of regulating and mitigating the negative spatial consequences of industrialization. In everyday life, a rich variety of community activities forms part of the glue that creates a coherent society. In Denmark, for instance, numerous associations provide some of the services one might expect to see provided by the state, and they also receive various kinds of public funding. Much organized sport, for children and for adults, is driven by local engagement and volunteer work in sport associations, which use public facilities and receive substantial public funding. The Christian church is also, to varying degrees and in various ways, interwoven with the public systems of the Nordic states.

Another fundamental factor behind the development of Nordic welfare planning is the level of trust: trust among people, and trust in the state. As pointed out by Svendsen (2018), trust in the state means that its public institutions are seen as trustworthy, so that people believe it will uphold every citizen's rights, regardless of their family situation, social status, or economic position; that it will provide and distribute welfare services with a fair yet firm hand; and that it will give each citizen the aid they need and are entitled to, such as access to a doctor or hospital, an education, and a pension in later life. Some may consider trust a vague, elusive concept, yet it has a huge impact on how we organize our lives and ourselves, including in spatial terms (Braae 2017). Gated communities barely exist in the Nordic countries, and open spaces are largely considered "public" spaces or commons, in the sense that they are freely accessible and open to everyone. Sweden and Norway share the concept of *allemansrätt* or *allemann-srett*, which gives everyone access to "the great outdoors", for example while walking or skiing – even across another person's property if it is open, uncultivated land. Arguably, this high degree of space-sharing is a prerequisite for trust, ensuring that people actually meet others who are unlike them.

The key term "welfare" has various semantic associations, depending on where you ask the question, of whom, and when. In the Nordic countries "welfare" denotes a way of organizing a society for the good of all, and it is an all-encompassing phenomenon. The Danish word for "welfare" (*velfærd*) is derived, and inverted, from the old phrase for "fare ye well" (*far vel*), used to wish someone a safe journey.[1] This can be seen as a parallel with one's journey through life. But *velfærd* also means "well-being" and is linked to the utilitarian credo of "the greatest good for the greatest number." Although the idea of maximizing public happiness is the democratically framed utopia of the welfare state, welfare is an ambiguous and dynamic concept (Wagenaar 2004). It can be understood either as a matter of satisfying needs, or as a matter of controlling resources. The first of these relates to Maslow's hierarchy of needs, where, in its simplest pyramidal form, the base comprises fundamental physical and security needs, with the need for love and appreciation in the middle and for self-realization at the top. The main challenge in this definition is that it depends on how contented a given individual is with their life situation, and moreover it turns the individual into a passive consumer of welfare goods. The second way of understanding welfare regards it as an infrastructure that can help the individual to control and direct their own life and living conditions, even in

1. In the modern Scandinavian languages, the word *farvel/farväl* simply means "goodbye"

the most concrete sense. The strong ideals and concepts of public happiness laid down for the new post-war (sub)urban communities were associated with the home and with public landscapes.

How to read this book

In the following chapters, these issues form the background against which I outline discussions that have taken place over several decades up to the present day. I go on to identify and describe the most relevant challenges facing urban planners today, and conclude with some reflections on future welfare planning – what it will encompass, and what direction it will take. My basic assumption is that the historically produced framework represents both the biggest challenge today *and* the potential for tomorrow's planning. The field itself focuses on planning the physical, spatial lifeworld of (sub)urban communities, which offers numerous things: a way to sustain health; a good everyday living environment with safe and efficient mobility; access to fresh air, light, and natural surroundings; a social life as part of larger networks; and a way to give each citizen influence over their lifeworld.

The book is divided into nine chapters, the next of which takes us back to the end of World War II and outlines a sequence of phases in the development of the welfare city and landscape. The two subsequent chapters specify the cross-scale dimension of welfare planning by considering the case of Copenhagen, zooming in on two levels: the regional and the everyday. This allows me to describe how physical planning transcends various scales – linking together national planning, regional planning, and local and site-specific planning – and how it consequently involves not only planners but also architects and landscape architects.

These three chapters form the historical backdrop for the next four. Each of these addresses a significant, current, and common Nordic challenge *to* the welfare city, partly caused *by* the welfare city. The major challenges are described by means of examples from the Nordic sphere. Chapter 5 discusses the housing crisis, focusing on Sweden and the polarization of rural and urban areas, the migration to metropolitan areas, and the lack of affordable housing. Chapter 6 explores social housing, which in many ways is the icon of a continued trend of segregation and increased inequity. Focusing on Denmark – by international standards a socially equitable country – and its "Ghetto Plan",[2] this chapter illustrates how the aim of engineering a socially mixed city unfolds in practice by remolding the social profile of its most problematic social housing estates. Chapter 7 addresses the compact city, moving to Oslo to shed light on the ongoing process of urban densification. This challenge is party related to the housing crisis described above, yet it also constitutes an independent phenomenon. In Chapter 8, I show how another shared challenge, climate change, is also affecting urban spatial planning. The case in point here is Copenhagen's 2012 "Cloudburst Plan", which aims to handle heavy rains and flooding, yet also seeks to make the Danish capital even more livable while securing valuable buildings and infrastructure, thereby providing long-term investor security.

Individually and together, these four crises – the shortage of affordable housing, the ghettoization of housing estates, the capitalization of city centers, and climate change – and the way they are handled have significant spatial impacts on the urban landscape. They are also very important from a planning perspective, both separately and in concert. They all imply changes within the existing urban fabric and challenge the Nordic welfare states' basic ideas of justice and equality, as well as their understanding of *what* welfare is embedded in material structures, and *for whom* that welfare is produced. Lastly – as will be addressed in the final chapter – they question how today's

2. The Danish word *ghetto*, which in modern usage has entered the language as a loan from English, denotes a neighborhood whose inhabitants typically earn low incomes and wield low social capital. Despite its negative connotations and ongoing debates in Denmark about the appropriateness of its use, it does not carry the same deep historical implications as the American English word

Chapter 2.

Nordic planning trajectories and steps towards the welfare city

The goals and values of what became known as "the welfare state" did not emerge ready-made. They were the result of a dynamic, open-ended development that was contested from several sides. As the literary scholar Lasse Horne Kjældgaard (2018) has recently shown, in Denmark these goals and values were subjected to considerable public debate among politicians, artists, and intellectuals, and were informed by events and practices outside of Denmark itself. During the formation of the Danish welfare state, there was an enormous cultural concern about defining the *meaning* of the term "welfare state". The connotations of the word "welfare" shifted from wealth (*velstand*) to well-being in the political appropriation of the logics of the universal welfare state model (Kjældgaard 2018: 47). Today many would argue that the pendulum has swung back, and the emphasis is now once again on wealth.

Here, our focus will mainly be on the materialization of the welfare state after World War II, the post-war period. Since the Danish post-war welfare city was initiated and structured by the state and was largely built as planned, we might expect buildings and landscapes from this period to mirror contemporary state values. Those state values developed in dialogue with the needs and interests expressed at ground level, and they were continually mediated through the designs and materializations produced by skilled planners and designers. This means that the dialogues revealed by Kjældgaard were both feeding into and influenced by the materialization of the welfare state. The dialogues that centered on the materialization itself – the planning and design of cities and landscapes – were informed by broad public discussions and by the discourse in and among professional circles. This intraprofessional discourse was multifaceted, as it addressed existing built works as well as newer subthemes and trends.

The post-war city was an extremely space-consuming phenomenon. More than half of Denmark's current building stock stems from the period after 1945, and if we compare the ground area occupied by these post-war built-up spaces with the total from the pre-war period, it becomes evident that the post-war segment takes up a far greater amount of land (Braae et al. 2020). While we do not have exact figures, the diagram of Greater Copenhagen suggests that the post-war built-up area covers roughly more than one and a half times (but not quite twice) the land area of the pre-war period. Although this observation is coarse-grained, we can conclude that the post-war city is very horizontal and very low-density. Looking more closely, we can also see that this low density results in a very green city. We might even say that the post-war city is a landscape city (Braae 2017).

The landscape played a highly constitutive role in the post-war city. It involved large, meticulously planned

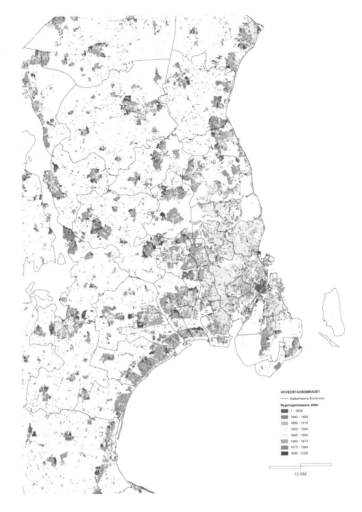

The vast post-war
urban expansion
The yellow, orange,
and red areas
were built up after
1945, and they
cover much larger
areas than the
other colors, which
show the building
activity of previous
periods.
© Dansk Bygnings-
arv / BARK

green spaces around public housing and institutions, as
well as private gardens around suburban homes. This was
echoed at the whole-city level, for example in the green
infrastructure built into Copenhagen's so-called Finger
Plan on a large scale, managing open space versus built-
up space, which will be the subject of Chapter 3. In some
cases, the landscape dimension was literally molded into
the spatial schemes of the building typology, which en-

compassed green open spaces, playing a significant cultural role.

The materialization of the welfare state involved several key undertakings. From the early post-war decades onward, housing was considered the main pillar of the materialization of the Danish welfare state (Bech-Danielsen et al. 2018), but education and administration, with the provision of new schools – elementary and high schools – and town halls, were also reflected the growing administrative apparatus and the redistribution of administrative centers. Furthermore, there were institutional buildings for the various age-specific new user groups that were directly sustained by the government, such as nurseries, kindergartens, and homes for the elderly. Moreover, the welfare city was geared towards a significant enlargement of industrial production: Large parcels of land were designated for industrial and business use, surrounded by plantations and situated next to significant highway infrastructure networks or far away from city centers.

Centralization and distribution

The differences in the Nordic countries' spatial planning ideals and practices include aspects of centralization versus decentralization, and hence of geographical distribution. The geography of both Norway and Sweden is largely defined by forests, mountains, and lakes, leading to an average population density of 12 people per square kilometer in Norway and 20 in Sweden. With its 126 people per square kilometer, Denmark has no mountains or large forests, and the population is more equally distributed over the whole area. Besides the geographical differences between the three Nordic countries, their economic situations and the national decisions they made after World War II greatly influenced their population distributions.

In Sweden, the migration from rural to urban areas and the ambition to raise the rural population's very low living standards led to centralization. In the decade before World War II, Sweden's farmers and other rural inhabitants were among the poorest in Europe, and by the 1930s approximately one million Swedes had emigrated to the United States. In 1964, the Swedish government decided to build a million new homes over a ten-year period, and indeed succeeded. More than 600,000 of the new dwellings were apartments in large-scale housing. Swedish planners regarded the existing cities as more or less fixed entities, resulting in the decision to construct several new satellite or "ABC" cities: "A" for *arbete* (work); "B" for *bostad* (housing); and "C" for *centrum* (center, meaning that each of these new settlements was to have its own city center). Early 1950s settlements such as Vällingby and Årsta served as models for the many new ABC satellite towns. Sweden's "Million Program" (*Miljonprogrammet*) entailed industrialized concrete construction, fueling the Swedish building industry. The appearance of concrete high-rise buildings changed the character of Swedish cities. What is more, as the Million Program sustained a rural exodus, it also changed the face of the country's rural areas. Over time the exodus led to the unintentional afforestation of vast tracts of former farmland, as land left uncultivated reverts to its natural state – which in Sweden's case is woodland.

Norway, on the other hand, took another path after World War II. At first, the Norwegian labor party (*Arbeiderpartiet*) aimed to run a planned economy, continuing the policy developed during the war. However, a combination of resistance from right-wing parties and a security policy alliance with the US kept Norway's capitalist economic system in place. In the 1970s, it began to extract substantial amounts of oil and gas from the North Sea, and this put the country's welfare-oriented economy on a different footing than was the case for Sweden or Denmark. Norway decided to use this new-found resource to aid its many remote and often very small settlements, including inland farming settlements, in parallel with the post-war urbanization and industrialization trends. The urbanization process in Norway focused more on providing infrastructure and planning for regional economic development, which took the shape of a decentralized realization of state policies. Planning decisions, too, were decentralized to reflect the local political majorities in the regional and municipal planning and building committees.

In Denmark, a third model was put to work after World War II. This was a hierarchical planning system that was meant to distribute all welfare services geographically, and accordingly, for several decades the national planning credo was "Denmark in balance". In the mid-1960s, national regional planning structured the whole country into A-, B-, and C-level cities. Unlike the Swedish "ABC" system, which referred to the cities' segregated functions, the Danish usage referred to an organizational structure that consisted of counties and municipalities. Within the municipalities (which, as local authorities, are two levels below the state), the A-level "town centers" and B- and C-level "service centers" were meant to connect the state or local public administration to the individual (Gudmand-Høyer et al. 2021). This system of distribution was also reflected in the transport infrastructure: highways, national roads, main roads, and neighborhood roads, often with cul-de-sac side streets and separate green pathways for cyclists and pedestrians. The hierarchy was fully installed with the Danish local government reform of 1970, which reduced the number of municipalities from 1,098 to 277 and the number of counties from 25 to 14. Essentially, the reform was meant as a remedy for the major towns that were spatially restricted by their municipal borders, and whose taxpayers were all in the lower-middle-class bracket. The aim was therefore to liberate the urban areas' potential in their new role as drivers of Denmark's industrialization, which in turn was to provide the funding for increased welfare through the production–consumption cycle.

The challenge in all three Scandinavian countries was to distribute universal welfare services equitably. Regardless of where they lived – in a remote village in the north, a city center, a new satellite city, or the core of an old city, every citizen was to have equal access to welfare services such as education and healthcare. However, these patterns of centralization and decentralization have changed substantially since the constitutive decades of early welfare state planning after World War II, and so have the aims and the means employed.

Development and preservation

Naturally, the urbanization process in the post-war era was extremely significant for welfare state planning. Momentous changes were taking place everywhere, and at high speed. Old city districts were demolished to make room for new infrastructures and new building complexes. Large parcels of former agricultural land were laid out for detached family houses, mass housing estates, and new city centers. Infrastructure networks of various kinds, from highways to residential cul-de-sacs, pedestrian walkways, and bicycle paths, were rolled out across the country, kilometer after kilometer of them, within a short period from the mid-1950s to the mid-1970s.

The countryside changed immensely in the two decades just after the war, too, thanks to the increased industrialization of agriculture. As mechanization progressed, the size of agricultural equipment increased, which led to the amalgamation of plots of land, the removal of hedgerows, and the draining of wetlands. The local government reform of 1970 was accompanied by mergers of agricultural properties and farms, and the number of full-time farms began to decline. According to the statistics, in 1960

New dreams of the good life become real
Key aspects of postwar dreams of the good life included plenty of green, open, naturalistic spaces for children and families, and high-quality housing. Here, the "Children's Lake" at the Fredhäll housing estate in Stockholm, designed by Oswald Almqvist in 1937. © Gullers, KW

Denmark had some 200,000 farms; in 2015 it had only 37,000. Even so, the proportion of Danish land used for agricultural purposes had been remarkably stable for decades, with around 66% of the total land area designated for agricultural use, in spite of the decreasing number of farming units, the growing cities, and the expanding infrastructure. Today, the share of land used for agriculture is approximately 62%. Denmark is the European country with the next-highest proportion of cultivated land measured by area, second only to Ireland.

The sweeping changes in both the urban and rural parts of the Nordic countries were accompanied by a new state apparatus set up to safeguard national heritage sites. This apparatus had been emerging since the early twentieth century; now it was set out in laws, and designated institutions were tasked with protecting national monuments from destruction. Nature conservation became an explicit priority in the urban development of the Greater Copenhagen area, and so did the listing of singular buildings. The latter was a mechanism put into place to avoid the demolition of old city centers, a frequent practice in the late 1960s to adapt inner cities to the increasingly heavy motor vehicle traffic. Gradually, however, heritage planning has shifted its focus from mere preservation, as seen earlier, to preservation partly through development.

Welfare city development phases

At the outset, Denmark apparently took the middle road compared with Sweden and Norway, which were archetypical examples, respectively, of centralization and decentralization. Nevertheless, all three of these Nordic countries' welfare systems and their spatial materialization have been subjected to ongoing interpretation, dismantling, demise, and dissolution on one hand, and to development, expansion, and concentration on the other. Over the years, several large Danish reforms have changed municipal borders, distributing and redistributing, centralizing and decentralizing areas of responsibility, as well as key institutions such as schools, residential care homes, town halls, and hospitals.[3] If we look at the development of the welfare city in Denmark, it can be roughly divided into five phases (Albertsen & Diken 2013).

The first phase, which ran from the end of World War II to the early 1970s, could be called *the Taylorist-Fordist-Keynesian-Corbusian phase*. Here we see the intertwining of the welfare state and the construction of the welfare city through state intervention, which aimed to fuel the reconstruction and re-industrialization that was an inherent part of the Marshall Aid plan. A utilitarianism of pure form was enacted in the architecture and urban planning of that period, based on the double and interdependent logic of production and consumption. The built environment was organized as a means of consumption *for* the public, funded *by* the public – meaning the state, the counties, and the municipalities. This consumption ideally

3. Examples are the 1970 "municipal reform" (*kommunalreformen*), the 2007 "structural reform" (*strukturreformen*), and the 2009 "quality reform" (*kvalitetsreformen*)

took place collectively, and much of it involved housing – social housing estates in parallel with single-family detached houses – as well as health, sport, leisure, education, and transportation facilities within the functionally segregated industrialized city. The city itself was very green and horizontal, low rise and low density, partly because about half of post-war construction resulted in single-family houses and was based on a centrifugal development logic, adding districts and new satellite settlements on the fringes of existing urban areas. A 1970 planning law divided Denmark's total land area into three types of zones – urban, rural, and "summer house" – the aim being to establish a clear-cut distinction between town/city areas and rural areas.[4]

The second phase, *the crisis of the utilitarian welfare city*, lasted for about ten years and became evident with the oil crisis in the early 1970s. The welfare state was in dire straits, and on an everyday level the crisis became very visible and concrete; for a while Danes were even prohibited from driving their cars on Sundays. The combined rise in unemployment and inflation neutralized the Keynesian policy of global demand management through deficit spending. In the words of the German political scientist and professor Christian Joppke, "The Keynesian welfare state has become the victim of its own success." The urbanization process slowed down, the many new apartments became difficult to rent out, and the guest workers who had come to Denmark to sustain the country's growing industrial production were often allocated housing on the newly built social housing estates.

The following decade, 1982-1992, can be labeled *the differentiated welfare cities phase*. Cities began competing with one another to attract successful workplaces, and thus wealthy taxpayers, operating within and at times beyond the national framework. Rather than being neutral infrastructures for the distribution of welfare goods and

4. Across the Nordic region the English term "city" is often used of urban entities that are quite small in global comparisons, but which are important to a region and usually have a university campus and a cathedral. An example would be Tromsø in Northern Norway, whose entire administrative area has a population of less than 80,000 (cf. Statistics Norway, www.ssb.no)

26

Greater Copenhagen, and with the completion in 2000 of the Øresund Bridge, which links Copenhagen by road and rail with Malmö in Sweden, the whole area on both sides of the sound became a new transnational growth region.

The status of cities as the main drivers of the economy, and the status of buildings as investment objects, became even more pronounced in the two to three decades that take us up to today, 2022. This is the fifth phase: *the competitive state and its competitive urban welfare landscape*. Spatial planning happens mainly through singular projects, and the urbanization process is guided by the prospect of investment payoffs. Even so, a sustainable urban development agenda has now started to gain ground. While environmental planning was a characteristic of the welfare state from the very beginning, ensuring clean water and promoting nature conservation, this phase shows an increasing emphasis on sustainable urban development. Here, the concept of the "compact city" appears to be a goal shared by advocates of sustainable urban development and developers alike. The neoliberal city embodies both perspectives, whether within the existing urban matrix or in new satellite districts, and it is seen as a favorable model by both private and public investors (Braae 2021). The municipalities play a dual role as local public authorities *and* investors, seeking to earn money by selling building options and attracting good, solid taxpayers. The neoliberal city is not a city as such, and it does not operate within the centrifugal urban development logic that previously characterized urban processes. Instead, it operates within the framework of existing cities, mainly from central locations such as former industrial estates and docklands. The neoliberal city fills in the "nooks and crannies" in the existing cityscape, or tears down parts of it, one after the other, and replaces them with new compact districts. Market-driven, neoliberal urban development takes place in attractively located areas close to the city center, offering grand views and efficient infrastructures. It is also dense, with a high percentage of built-up area, meaning that the ground is paved, and it benefits from access to existing open spaces. Finally, the neoliberal city does not follow any overall plan for either urban or regional development, and while all its buildings may meet various sustainability standards, the environmental contribution of this kind of urban development is highly questionable.

Chapter 3.

Planning with green open spaces in Denmark

To sustain an urban entity, one must be able to control its metabolism: the influx of water, energy, food, and so on, and the outflow of waste. This requires planning of how the city's territory is organized and managed, which in turn must take into account green open spaces and the benefits they bring to the inhabitants. With Copenhagen, the capital of Denmark, as my main example, this chapter focuses on the coming-into-being of the physical and spatial framework that underlies today's urban planning challenges. This coming-into-being was a multi-scaled materialization of post-war welfare thinking. Organizationally, it ranged from state to county to municipality, reflecting the planning that took place on a national, regional, and municipal/local level. Spatially, it unfolded in the planning of green open spaces, taking place along a spectrum that extended from the regional scale at one end to the public spaces by people's curbside doorsteps at the other. This last and smallest scale is the focus of the next chapter. The linkage *across* scales is a key feature, which in a Danish context can be specifically exemplified by connecting the green wedges of the capital's extensive metropolitan "Finger Plan" with an armchair in a bay window overlooking a lawn on a large housing estate. In this sense, Copenhagen is a remarkable case: It strongly embodies and materializes spatial ideas about welfare, their embeddedness in green open spaces, and how their use and appearance has changed over time. Meanwhile, the idea of integrating parks into the urban layout is also a key factor in the urbanization that took place from the late 1800s and for several decades after that, across Western Europe and North America. Likewise, we see certain cross-national similarities in the 1920s and 1930s, when green open systems were united and expanded to form entire park networks that were integrated into the urban plan. Sweden, with its Stockholm Parks Department led by Oswald Almquist, was the first country in Europe to develop a modern park system, and in the post-war period these efforts were pursued to their fullest extent by his successor, Holger Blom. In Norway, the Oslo park director Marius Røhne and the planning director Harald Hals did not collaborate directly, yet they worked towards the same goals and both emphasized "the virtues and advantages of having green spaces blended into the urban structure" (Jørgensen & Thorén 2013).

Free and equal access to nature Both in practical and ideological terms, access to green open spaces is a common denominator for leisure landscape planning in the Nordic welfare states. © Torben Nielsen

A landscape response to urbanization

In Copenhagen, the urbanization that took place from the late nineteenth century onwards was manifested as "layer upon layer" of buildings, working from the old city center outwards, and stretching into new suburbs that sometimes appeared to be an incongruous and haphazard urbanization of otherwise beautiful landscapes. The living conditions in the inner city were poor, sanitation was inadequate, and its daily functioning was constrained by congestion. Traffic management was a major issue, but the

fact that more and more citizens had more and more leisure time was also a growing concern. The layered expansion of the city gradually came to cover a large geographical area, which made it increasingly difficult to reach the
open land and recreational areas outside Copenhagen. In
parallel, the citizens of the new suburbs also needed access to these areas. Paradoxically, the new and growing
suburbs themselves diminished the extent of these recreational areas and in some cases even prevented public access to them. Privately owned, fenced-off parcels of land
were situated right down to the beach along the coastline
north and south of Copenhagen, and the lakes and wooded
areas in the northern reaches of the city were also slowly
being encircled by private housing, again fencing off these
blue-green islands from public access. Some of the new
satellite towns were extended deep into the open countryside, with areas of detached single-family housing.

In the 1920s, discussions about how to organize traffic gave rise to the idea that traffic lines could be integrated into the suburban municipalities' planning activities, thereby offering a first step towards overall urban planning across municipal borders in a large part of the capital region. Regional planning work was finally initiated in 1928 with the appointment of a planning committee for the Copenhagen region (Vejre 2016). Remarkably, their first move was to set up a subcommittee that would focus on green open spaces, which ultimately resulted in the 1936 "Green Report". In this way the capital's administrators put the traffic and congestion issues on hold for a while to concentrate on developing a landscape-based foundation to support the future development of Copenhagen and the region more generally – which makes the approach to Copenhagen's urbanization process more radically landscape-based than parallel processes in the other two Scandinavian countries.

The impetus behind the new green subcommittee was to work out a park policy that could guide future planning. Extensive natural areas would be of the utmost importance for the region's future citizens, their outdoor activities, their recreation, and what was referred to as "the people's educational and pedagogical use" of green spaces. Such ideas had a strong following in this period due to the massive migration from the countryside to the swelling towns and cities, which also created an emerging working class. The idea of a park policy built around a regional system of green open spaces was promoted in the 1920s by G. N. Brandt (1878-1945), a well-read scholar and the head of parks and gardens in the exclusive municipality of Gentofte (north of Copenhagen). This policy rested on the principle of remote recreational areas that would benefit everyone, "for the common good," organized in a cohesive park system spanning the entire metropolitan region. This park system was to include the metro area's existing bogs, lakes, groves, and forests, which were to be interlinked by green parkways, bicycle lanes, and footpaths. Instead of urbanizing in concentric circles, layer upon layer, a set of roads radiating like wheel spokes would guide the urbanization to follow its lines. This new logic would make it possible to keep green wedges intact between the radiating suburban belts. The wedges would preserve existing agricultural land and provide room for specific recreational areas. Moreover, the radiating spokes of parkland would be complemented by parkland belts that ran across the radiating urban lines, spinning a web of green spaces throughout the metropolitan region (Vejre 2016).

The areas that were to form the new coherent park system would either be bought by public authorities or listed as nature conservation areas. In both cases it would be possible, firstly, to prevent them from being urbanized and, secondly, to give the general public access to them. These concepts converged with the ongoing debates about nature conservation. In the early twentieth century, nature conservation was based on scientific and aesthetic values that did not specifically include any recreational aspect. Later, a social dimension related to the recreational value of nature became fully integrated, which was manifested in the 1917 Nature Protection Act. This legislation was promoted by the Danish Society for Nature Conservation, which became a collaboration partner in the long period of regional development planning that followed. In other words, at the beginning of the twentieth century the pressures from Danish urbanization became increasingly clear, and planning initiatives at the time worked out radical plans to protect landscapes (Vejre 2016). As we will see, throughout this period the question of making landscapes accessible to the public at large took on a new urgency.

The 8-8-8 schedule and a leisure culture

In the early twentieth century, leisure time (apart from Sundays and holidays) was a privilege reserved for the upper classes: the nobility, the wealthy, and senior officials and executives in public and private enterprises. Then, in 1919, the eight-hour workday became the new norm (Bro 2016). This led to the "8-8-8 schedule", which divided the day into three parts of equal size: eight hours of work, eight hours of rest, and eight hours of (relative) freedom. Over the following decades, paid holidays also became a common right; in 1938 Denmark decreed by law that all workers were to have at least two weeks' holiday per year, with full pay.

For ordinary people, having more free time meant that their lives could include leisure - beyond cooking, cleaning, staying warm, washing and mending clothes, procuring everyday necessities, and doing all the other ordinary tasks involved in day-to-day living. Many spent part of their free time on entertainment, going to cinemas and restaurants; another part of it on self-improvement activities like visiting the public library, attending lectures, taking courses, or attending evening classes (*aftenskole-undervisning*); and yet another part contributing to one or more of the numerous associations and clubs that began to appear, especially for youth activities and sports.

The workers' movement, which was the main force behind the limitation of working hours, regarded leisure time as a social question of the utmost importance (Bro 2016: 157). Free time served three functions for wage-earners in factories, offices, shops, and warehouses. First, it allowed workers to rest, counteracting the physical fatigue caused by their work. Secondly, it could compensate for the monotony and lack of personal development and satisfaction that repetitive work entailed. Third, it had a psychological function, which was to provide peace and relaxation to counteract the stress of the noisy, high-speed environment, urban life in general, and the economic and social uncertainty that followed migrating from a rural to an urban lifestyle. As a result of this logic, the politically influential workers' movement took a moral and, to some extent, instrumental stance on the "reasonable" or "suitable" use of leisure time. As commercial mass culture was believed to pacify people, it was regarded as inappropriate. Instead, the active use of leisure time was closely related to cultural activities and cultural consumption more widely. The development of culture, and thus of democratic culture per se, was considered to be dependent on people's everyday use of their leisure time. In other words, there was a strong link between the individual person and society at large. On the one hand, ideally, leisure time ought to be experienced as meaningful by each and every person; on the other, leisure time was the best tool to "raise up" the lower social classes and, in a wider perspective, to increase equity and diminish social differences (Bro 2016).

In Denmark, society was responsible for providing the framework within which each individual could fulfill their role. It did this by giving the lower and middle classes equal access to opportunities for physical and intellectual development; by distributing cultural goods more equally; and by ensuring broad and equal access to leisure and cultural activities. The aim was not to create special domains or preserves for the working class, but to establish the basis for a common cultural sphere that could include various social classes. This was closely linked to the landscape, which offered the perfect spatial setting for this kind of culture.

Leisure time spent in the open air was given high priority. While preparing the 1917 Nature Protection Act, leading social-democratic politicians explicitly proposed that "open-air culture" for all Danish citizens be made an integral part of the future welfare society. This was also a matter of distributing national resources more equitably, as many natural areas had been privatized due to the ongoing industrialization and urbanization. New groups of wealthy citizens had arisen, manifesting their position and developing their cultural habits by building large villas in attractive areas – which, by this time, were within easy reach of the masses, thanks to the advent of automobiles and expanding infrastructure. Among other things, the Nature Protection Act was meant to provide ordinary people with access to open areas – "free nature", as it was called in everyday language. The main argument was that such access was a necessary amenity for workers living in crowded inner-city apartment blocks with no direct sunlight, as many of the newly arrived previously rural people did. Initially this argument was linked to social class, but it gradually took on a more universal ring: *Everyone* deserved to have access to green open spaces, and so the aim remained unchanged.

When the Nature Protection Act was revisited in 1937, the aim had shifted: Now, it was meant to link humans and nature within a national framework. The Danish politician Julius Bomholt (1896–1969) – who later became the driving force behind the creation of the country's Ministry of Culture, and served as its first minister – argued that the government ought to make these attractive parts of the Danish landscape accessible to the people by law (under the motto "Denmark for the people"). In his view, the task of maintaining access to uncultivated areas of land obviously fell to the public authorities, the state, and the municipalities (Bro 2016: 163). The Danish prime minister at the time, the social-democratic legend Thorvald Stauning (1873–1942), was dedicated to nature conservation and open access across class boundaries, and he believed the law ought to expand society's right to conserve nature for the common good of the entire population. In 1935 he had shifted the administrative responsibility for nature conservation from the Ministry of Justice to his own department, the Ministry of State. In his view, nature was a place where one could withdraw, a refuge for physical development, and a setting in which to improve health and culture. Nature consequently became the spatial framework where everyone could spend time and find something entertaining to do, or exercise or relax, regardless of social class. The natural environment was also seen as a setting that could counteract cultural differences, a task at which traditional types of "high culture" had not succeeded. Lastly, nature was a refuge from the urban environment and its monotonous, alienating lifestyles.

The notion of leisure landscapes was now present in the public debate, and some of the key listings of natural areas were finalized before World War II. The new and growing leisure culture had significant implications for planning at all levels. So did the many new "user groups" that emerged in parallel with the growth of the welfare state and its responsibilities. In particular, children and the elderly came to receive much attention in the planning and design of the welfare city and its leisure and housing areas.

The Green Report and the Finger Plan

As previously mentioned, the Green Report of 1936 paved the way for a large-scale urban development plan from 1947 officially called *Fingerplanen*, "the Finger Plan", so called because its shape looked like a hand, with fingers spread, placed on a map of Greater Copenhagen. The older part of the city was covered by the palm, while the new suburbs were organized along the five fingers. The areas in between, the green wedges identified in the Green Report, were described by some as a "green crown" or "green glove". These two images defined one another, and yet they were also an arena where a drawn-out battle raged. In subsequent decades, the development of adequate man-

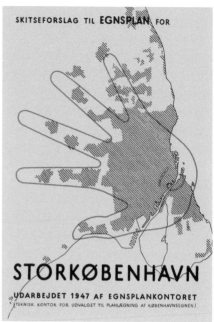

SKITSEFORSLAG TIL **EGNSPLAN** FOR

STORKØBENHAVN

UDARBEJDET 1947 AF EGNSPLANKONTORET
(TEKNISK KONTOR FOR UDVALGET TIL PLANLÆGNING AF KØBENHAVNSEGNEN)

agement tools became a major administrative problem. For quite a long time, the main tool to safeguard the dividing line between the built-up areas and the green open areas was nature conservation legislation. But the race between conservation and urbanization was intense, and by 1970 or so, roughly 50% of the planned green wedge areas had been urbanized (Vejre et al. 2016: 398).

Physical planning is a way to balance various interests. Denmark's post-war planning balanced the three general tasks of conserving nature, protecting aesthetically valuable landscapes, and providing a new spatial framework to meet the increasing demand for open-air activities. It did this by developing housing, industry, infrastructure, and supply lines; in the post-war period, the pressure on housing as well as industry and infrastructure was immense. The Finger Plan aimed to distribute Copenhagen's urban development in various directions, thereby

Green spaces and
plans to build go
hand in hand
The Green Report
(left) laid the
foundation for the
urban development
Finger Plan (right)
and still serves
today as "the green
glove" of the Finger
Plan for the greater
Copenhagen area,
although it is
constantly being
challenged by new
urban development
proposals set in its
green wedges.
© Dansk Byplan-
laboratorium

avoiding the concentric layer-upon-layer logic that had prevailed. In essence, the plan sought to avoid increasing the distance between residential areas and recreational areas, and to ensure mobility. These aims were also indirectly informed by the wartime experience of the surface bombing of dense cities – hence the wish to avoid vulnerable, densely packed hubs. The pattern of the Finger Plan was regarded as the best possible solution to steer future urban development in the desired direction, taking into account that demographics and patterns of business and transportation could develop in various ways.

Urban areas and industrial areas were also included within the Finger Plan's urbanized region, but they were kept apart. The bone of each finger in the plan was an "S-train" railway line and a main road. The green wedges were defined as recreational areas or agricultural areas that would be part of the food supply or, alternatively, might be needed for other purposes in the future. Agricultural areas nearby were considered to be of recreational value, and the distances between the plan's urbanized areas and green open spaces were very short.

Topography came to play a significant role in the capital's urbanization process. The landscape north of Copenhagen is undulating, with many lakes and relatively large wooded areas. In fact, the whole of North Zealand is greatly appreciated for its natural beauty, and is an attractive place to settle. The long coastline south of Copenhagen is considered attractive for the same reasons, while the landscape to the west is flat, with no woodlands, lakes, or other significant topographical features. This lack of interesting natural landscapes called for the construction of new recreational destinations. A special effort would have to be made to ensure future urban development in this part of the Finger Plan. The earliest ideas suggested a web-like system of green corridors. These were gradually replaced by an idea to partially mold the terrain and create

Chapter 4.
Everyday welfare landscapes

In the Nordic countries of the post-war period, the notion of "the good life" was synonymous with equal access to good-quality housing, well-paid jobs, and education. The urban framework for this idea built upon a cluster of values: housing for all; healthy, just, and democratic cities; strong communities; and (as spelled out in the Finger Plan, discussed in Chapter 3) equal and easy access to nature, as well as a good environment in which to raise children. Other aspects of the post-war welfare city's programming were achieved in large part through green open spaces, which many saw as synonymous with the good life, and which operated as "landscapes for living". In other words, it was by no means accidental that planners at the more detailed level decided to locate mass housing estates in green environments, and to sculpt those landscapes with huge lawns and dedicated spaces for play and recreation, in contrast to the industrial city's dense, dark, and unsanitary residential neighborhoods. Yet this decision was more than just a reaction against the industrial city, as it stood on the shoulders of both social reformers and urban utopians who had focused on public health and sanitation early. Perhaps we hear echoes of the *Lebensreform*, the early twentieth-century vitalist current that emphasized nature's healing, constitutive, and emancipative power. On a more fundamental level, we can look back to the natural sciences of the nineteenth century and scientists such as Ernst Haeckel (1834-1919), who put forward the concept of "ecology", which describes how an organism relates to its external world. This perspective was translated by social scientists and early planners into a way of conceptualizing the relationship between a human community and its social, political, economic, and not least physical milieu or lifeworld – that is, a community shaping and being shaped by its environment (Haffner 2021: 2-3).

The embedded landscapes of social housing

While the Danish Finger Plan's green wedges provided a large-scale framework of remote recreational areas, welfare ideas were also embedded in everyday open spaces. As in the Finger Plan, such spaces were decided upon by the public administration, paid for with public funding, and planned and designed *by* the public *for* the public. This clear relationship between political ideas of welfare (and thus state administration) and the materialization of those ideas was spelled out particularly clearly in the social housing estates' green open spaces. They were constructed in parallel with thousands and thousands of detached single-family houses, each on its own plot, gathered in large, carpetlike districts separated by spacious green areas and infrastructure. Today, such detached single-family houses are popular with the Danes, but it is worth remembering that social housing is also a prominent housing type.

Seen from an international perspective, social housing can be quite diverse. In some countries, such as the US, social housing is subsidized residential accommodation administered by federal, state, or local agencies for low-income households, almost inextricably links it with the lower socio-economic classes. In Switzerland, the provision of housing is market-based, and there is no national policy for providing affordable or social housing. In the Nordic countries, social housing was originally meant for everyone. Norway is generally market-based, and around 80% of its population are homeowners, either through individual ownership or as part of cooperative housing arrangements, leaving a small, mostly private rental sector. The members of Norwegian cooperative housing estates buy shares that grant them the right to occupy a specific home. In Sweden, three million people (out of the country's ten million) live in rented accommodation, half of which is public housing built as part of the Million Program, mentioned earlier and treated later in this book. In Denmark, some one million people (out of about six million) live on social housing estates, which make up just under half of the total segment of rental homes (40%). The Danish non-profit housing sector is subject to municipal supervision, and municipalities have the right to allocate one quarter of all social housing units to tenants of their choosing. This segment is legally defined as affordable and decent housing for those who need it, and to give the tenants a legal and decisive right to influence their own living conditions (Rogaczewska et al. 2014).

Danish social housing estates can be understood as ensembles of buildings and open spaces. At the time of their construction, they were internationally acclaimed for their architectural and spatial qualities. These qualities related to the prevailing ideas of welfare at the time, and to the fact that such estates were the result of close collaborations among landscape architects, architects, and planners. Their design foregrounded the landscape's embedded welfare values as a complex relational construct (Braae et al. 2020). This meant that they interlinked the spatial appearance of the estate with other spheres of

everyday life, forged connections to other parts of the welfare city, and created a dialogue between disproportionate
or even dialectically opposed elements such as nature and
culture, process and form, and land and life.

Access to nature was a solid pillar in the materialization of the welfare state in all the Nordic countries, and
so was housing. Indeed, housing has been said to be the
main pillar, and much effort was put into planning and
building it. The combination of the two pillars was a logical
step, and the landscape dimension was literally molded
into the estates' spatial schemes; housing was the sphere
most closely related to everyday human life, and thus to
the question of what welfare meant on an individual level.
In essence, we can identify three spatial relationships
(Braae et al. 2020). The first is called the *pastoral scenery or park settlement*, where single housing blocks and
towers are situated in an open park with lawns as the uni-

Three ways to relate in spatial terms to landscapes and housing These three housing estates – from left Bellahøj (1951–1957), Albertslund Syd (1963–1968), and Farum Midtpunkt (1970–1974) – originated in three different decades and demonstrate three ways of molding together the landscape and the built-up volumes. © Jessen/ Welland

5. Brutalism is an architectural style from the 1950s and 1960s, typified by a clear exhibition of structure and mainly done in prefabricated elements of cast concrete

fying element, as seen around the Bellahøj social housing estate (1951–1957) in Denmark. This parallels the modernist spatial code of objects placed on a coherent surface. Many housing estates from the decades just after World War II are organized according to this layout. The second spatial relationship is *the structural pattern*, a low-rise, high-density way of organizing built-up spaces and open spaces. This model – of which the Albertslund Syd estate (1963–1968) in Denmark is a good example – can be seen as a critique of the alienation engendered by the often large-scale pastoral scenery. The third spatial relationship between built-up volumes and open spaces is that of *topographic megastructures*, with a layering or terracing of the two parts. This model is used less often, but it occurs in some Brutalist housing estates,[5] such as Farum Midtpunkt (1970–1974); it has recently started to reappear, for example in the housing estate of Bjerget (2008) in the Ørestad region.

Although open spaces are associated with numerous values related to their appearance, meaning, and use, they have been amalgamated into both explicit and implicit ideas of welfare. Moreover, their role is highly ambiguous. On the one hand, the various welfare landscapes relate to specific contexts, such as a particular housing estate or public institution, and they therefore function as common spaces for specific, defined groups of people. On the other hand, they are to a certain degree considered part of a wider public sphere and consequently make up various kinds of public space. This ambiguity, and the nuances embedded in the distinction between common space and public space, is one of the key points in the currently ongoing transformation of Danish social housing estates. If we follow the British urbanist Gordon Cullen (1977: 128), who spelled out the critiques of the modernist spatial scheme, the communal space - the space that belongs to all of us - is the "floor" or the ground: the most basic thing of all. Despite his general critique of what he labeled modernist "prairie planning" and its focus on transportation, which led to the fragmentation of the floor, he still foregrounded the floor's unifying, accessible, and democratizing role as "the common surface". This allowed the practice of "the right of free assembly" and the right to "enjoy the pleasure of being sociable" (Cullen 1977: 128).

The open spaces that are integral parts of social housing estates work as a commons-like surface, and are often green. Since the late nineteenth century, housing estates have focused on the human being's relationship with nature. The idea of the garden city was developed around 1900 by the British urban planner Ebenezer Howard, who focused on the connection between the garden and the individual dwelling, whether in the form of the detached single-family house or in smaller units of several households. This was an active relationship; as the garden was just outside the main door, it had to be cultivated, and it constituted a private unit. A few decades later, the International Congress for Modern Architecture (CIAM) movement emphasized the role of collective green open spaces, which, on the contrary, were to be seen from a distance and did not require individual involvement (Braae 2021). Citizens would have the pleasure of being in natural surroundings, but they were to be liberated from the burden of tilling the land. This double perspective – being *free to* access nature, and yet also being *free from* depending on nature – was the basis for literally building the landscape into post-war housing plans, and it became integral to ideas about how to house people. Social housing construction programs were structured as multiple-apartment blocks situated in a common landscape – that is, amid pastoral scenery. This spatial relationship aimed to do more than just ensure direct sunlight into dwellings or onto the ground between the apartment blocks, and equally to do more than just provide people with something green to look at from their individual dwellings or while coming and going. The landscape was a remote recreational feature, but at the same time, when directly integrated into the housing scheme, it provided a new set of human relationships that expanded the content of *what* could be associated with welfare and *for whom*.

Chaining recreational space

The new architecture developed by socially engaged architects sought to relate the interior of the home with the exterior, and this became a prominent feature of modernist architecture from the 1920s onwards. The interiors of the large-scale housing estate dwellings and the green open spaces outside met in a new architectural element: the bay window or balcony. This, however, was only the first link in a chain of interconnected open spaces, which opened onto one another at ever-higher levels in the scalar hierarchy. The green open space below the apartment was linked to the landscape of the whole estate, which in turn was linked to nearby sports fields, linked in their turn to green wedges on the regional scale, like those found in the Greater Copenhagen Finger Plan.

Although the integrated landscape may look natural, it is far from a neutral backdrop. Nowadays we may take the appearance of the landscape for granted, but it was not a given in the post-war decades. At that time, social housing in Denmark and across Europe became a means for testing new modes of living, based on the assumption that the landscape held transformative potential. The landscape as a fully shared commons, as prescribed by CIAM, gradually came to feature elements that would support individual use, such as terraces and balcony gardens. In the 1980s, following the criticism of modernist planning schemes and architecture, the new "dense-low" (*tæt-lav*) social housing type took this thinking to its extreme, working with a detailed zoning system to designate areas within a given housing estate for public/semi-public/semi-private/private use. This zoning-based design approach downscaled the landscape, even while maintaining its key role as a common ground and a prerequisite for the good life.

Ideas of community

Ideas of the good life were also closely related to ideas about communities (Wagenaar 2004). Although the social-democratic welfare state models in the Nordic countries created a direct relationship between the individual and the state, various kinds of communities were imagined on multiple scales. They ranged from abstract and ethical configurations that took shape in green open spaces and gently rolling landscapes to very literally concrete and practical needs. As the well-known and highly influential Danish architect and urban planner Steen Eiler

Rasmussen (1898–1990) put it while designing the innovative Tingbjerg housing estate (1958–1971): "The human being is first and foremost a social being, and in order for the individual to thrive and develop, he must feel contact with others, learn from others, influence as much as be influenced by others" (Rasmussen 1963: 21). The nation, as embodied by the state, could be seen as a community: one that was held together by taxes, policies, and equally distributed welfare goods. However, as the emergent hierarchical model produced new conceptions of community, housing estates provided a framework for multi-scaled communities organized around space and spatial functions.

Children and childhood more generally were gaining attention, and green open spaces were relevant to both. At the intersection of Rasmussen's writings and works, we find detailed descriptions of how he envisioned the role of green welfare from cradle to grave. For many years Rasmussen worked closely with the prominent Danish landscape architect Carl Theodor Sørensen (1893–1979), with whom he also developed Tingbjerg, a new, large housing estate set in a picturesque natural environment on Greater Copenhagen's northwestern perimeter. Its landscaping became an important identity marker and an integral part of the project.

On the Tingbjerg estate, which Rasmussen (1963: 5) called a "society of human beings", the relationships between housing and landscape represented a meticulously thought-out structure that sought to ensure the well-being of all who lived there, offering differentiated living arrangements for people of all ages and classes. Rasmussen's humanism is an example of post-war urban planning's optimism and its conviction that it really was possible to plan for a better society. This conviction had been shared by modernist planning, but Rasmussen's work went beyond the prevailing idea that the house ought to be a "machine

for living in", as formulated by the celebrated modernist architect Le Corbusier. Despite the deliberately humble appearance of Tingbjerg's architecture – which celebrated everyday architecture and human equality – the concepts underlying its design ethos formed a complex web of sometimes contested priorities, such as welfare, nature, culture, individual, community, state, artist, citizen, past, present, and future.

Designed to ensure the well-being of citizens of all ages, the social-democratic welfare state model rested on the principle that everyone should be assured the right to receive social welfare services, regardless of their class or their family's ability to take care of them. Children's ability to develop into civic-minded, well-functioning adults had to be nurtured by stimulating their physical lifeworld. This

The junkyard playground
A Danish invention, the "junkyard playground" was designed as a counterweight to the spatial constraints and the slum-like housing conditions of the inner city, creating spaces where children's imagination could be given free rein.
© Sven Türck / VISDA

was a qualitative kind of well-being, premised upon the idea of the individual developing in a context where freedom was constantly held in check by the self-regulating social norms of the wider community - rather than by the family, as in the communitarian welfare state model, or by formal educators, as in the liberal welfare state model.

Rasmussen (1963: 21-30) took his cue from 1930s reformist ideas about education and pedagogy, which questioned the prevailing wisdom that adults needed to force knowledge into children, and which drew inspiration from Rousseau's idea of natural development. Childhood was considered a complex phenomenon, with several developmental stages. Older children ought to have the opportunity to be left to their own devices and build their own playhouses out of "junk", developing their own democracy and using play as a tool - an idea that Tingbjerg's landscape architect, Sørensen, had already spelled out in 1940 in his internationally recognized concept of the "junkyard playground" (*skrammellegeplads*), where children could build and play in real structures using scrap materials (Gutman & de Coninck-Smith 2008). Rasmussen acknowledged each step of child development, and he constructed a differentiated open space design, envisioning the estate's open spaces as one big playscape for children (and adults) of various ages. Green open spaces directly embedded ideas of well-being into the plans for Tingbjerg. However, there was a huge difference in how children and adults related to the welfare landscape in Rasmussen and Sørensen's design, as the involvement of adults was mostly based on sharing services, culture, and consumption, and on a more contemplative and passively consuming relationship in which the green open spaces served as places for encounters and recreation.

What we have seen is that green open spaces were just as highly constitutive for welfare production from a near-home perspective as they were in the large-scale ur-

Chapter 5.
The Swedish housing crisis

Sweden is currently going through a housing crisis that is manifesting as a shortage of housing, specifically affordable housing. It is also manifesting in a dysfunctional housing market with social segregation that clusters the most vulnerable classes together; in increased inequity, like a pyramid with a small, very wealthy top and a large base; in a highly indebted middle class; and in the precarious working conditions of the new generations, who cannot enter the housing market. The nature of the Swedish housing crisis is financial and social – and, one might add, related to urban planning. It highlights a key dimension of the formation of welfare states and their bureaucracy and planning apparatus, namely housing provision. Sweden is not exceptional. Some characteristics of the Swedish housing crisis can be found elsewhere, including in the other Nordic countries, which share some of the major forces that drive and challenge them in providing sound, healthy, accessible, and affordable housing. Nevertheless, each national context is unique by virtue of the country's legacy and its economic and legal framework, and the situation also differs from city to city, and even from district to district. Below, I go into more detail about the Swedish housing crisis, but first we need to understand the challenge in the general context of welfare planning, in the historical context, and in terms of the role of social housing in Sweden.

Housing – a wobbly pillar?

Following World War II, housing was considered the main pillar in the materialization of the welfare state and the contract between the state and its citizens (Swenarton et al. 2014). As described in Chapter 1, building new housing was necessary given the number of people left homeless after the war, but it was also a way of fueling the long-planned industrialization process. As part of this new industrialization, housing was needed for the many people who had previously worked in the agricultural sector. A distinct aspect of the Nordic welfare model described by Esping-Andersen is that besides new housing, the welfare society also had to provide kindergartens for children and care homes for the elderly. These developments in the Nordic model happened in parallel with women entering the labor market, and with the home and family losing their status as informal, decentralized social institutions that provided care to all family members, across generations. The new dwellings were designed mostly to accommodate what became the new family norm, "the nuclear family" consisting of two parents and two children.

Housing provision after World War II went beyond the various welfare state models, but the methods and mechanisms used to bring it about varied enormously – even in the Nordic region, where all the countries were democratic welfare states. Despite the differences in the various forms of social rental housing that developed throughout Europe during the post-war decades, they succeeded in many ways. Rented social housing provided homes for millions of people, produced socially equitable

56

outcomes, and alleviated the severe lack of housing resulting from the war and from underinvestment. It significantly improved the overall living standards of mainstream working households, fostering upward mobility (Blackwell & Bengtsson 2021: 2).

Social housing

Large-scale housing estates constructed during the building boom that occurred around 1960–1975 are an almost omnipresent feature of European cities. Today, millions of people, often with very diverse backgrounds, live in such large-scale housing estates, which offer an alternative to the accelerating rent hikes and financialization of other urban areas. In the Nordic countries social housing plays a special role, and it continues to provide homes for a large part of the Nordic populations. The social housing systems in Sweden and Denmark are the most significant. Yet despite the success of the Nordic "social housing associations" and their significant contributions to society, their perceived status, and that of similar systems elsewhere, remains ambiguous, shifting, and at the margins of the welfare state. Indeed, this is so prevalent that some have labeled housing "the wobbly pillar under the welfare state" (Blackwell & Bengtsson 2021). Not surprisingly, the social housing system has come under fire.

Social rental housing cannot be seen in isolation; it is an integral part of a society's housing provision in general. It is operated to meet housing needs, rather than to make a profit for a landlord. This core function entails at least three attributes. First of all, it implies an ethos of meeting housing needs based on non-profit principles, which crucially distinguishes social rentals from private ones. Secondly, social rental housing in the Nordic countries is also characterized by high standards in terms of spaciousness, furnishings and amenities, and the local environment. Finally, it ensures tenant security, in terms of both formal

From housing deficit to housing surplus
The Million Program (1965–1974) came in many scales – here the two-story Smedby estate north of Stockholm. Despite its success – providing 1,000,000 new dwellings in less than ten years – the many large-scale social housing estates became home to the two groups with the lowest incomes, even as the middle class gained new opportunities.
© Ellen Braae

and real protection of residents from eviction and from rent hikes which, in practice, would force them to leave their homes. These general functions and properties apply to social rental housing in many European countries, but they are delivered, challenged, changed, and managed in many different ways.

For most of the second half of the twentieth century the rental system governing Swedish social housing attracted "wonder and admiration" (Blackwell 2021: 338), as the darling of the housing world. Timothy Blackwell, a Swedish housing researcher, describes the core functions of Swedish social rental housing as a system of municipal housing companies (MHCs) which in the 1930s and 1940s became directly involved with government housing policy (Blackwell & Bengtsson 2021). The politicians wanted to achieve a universal housing policy: *allmännyttan*, literally meaning "the common good", and in this context "the public housing sector". By means of state loans directed towards all forms of tenure, the MHCs were supposed to balance housing production and management in parallel with private housing. The nationwide shortage of afford-

general election in 2021 was highly affected by the housing crisis, which therefore spilled over into a political crisis.

In 2020, 70% of local authorities in Sweden reported a housing shortage, the average waiting time for rent-controlled housing being nine years (Reuters 2021). Many tenants find their homes on the black market, on contracts at much higher prices than are normal and with no legal rights. Parallel to this, house prices have increased, partly encouraged by generous mortgage tax deductions aimed at promoting property purchases. This has left Swedish households with unprecedented levels of debt; currently they are among the most indebted in Europe. Young and first-time homebuyers are incurring more mortgage debt than previous generations, and this has reached such a high level that it is threatening the Swedish economy and weakening the fabric of society. This situation makes it extremely difficult to enter the housing market, which is exacerbated by the fact that the framework of younger generations' working conditions is shifting towards fixed-term, insecure employment. The situation is a catch-22: members of the growing precariat have nowhere to live if they want to stay in the cities, which is where the jobs are. Moreover, the lower middle class cannot afford to live in the large conurbations, making it difficult for schoolteachers, nurses, police officers, and people in similar occupations to live within an acceptable distance of their workplaces. Statistics show that the wealthiest have more space than before, while the lowest-income groups live closer together (Mouratidis 2022). The social housing estates have increasingly become home to low-income groups, a large proportion of whom may be second- or third-generation immigrants, adding a cultural dimension to the social segregation. Furthermore, these low-income groups are unable to mobilize and have become spatially segregated. They may be marginalized on the labor market as well, adding to their segregation and residualization. Some of the social housing estates appear to be remote enclaves, a perception sustained by the infrastructural ideals in play at the time of their construction, which favored the estate as a self-contained entity on its own, rather than as a fully integrated part of the urban fabric, infrastructurally and functionally. Simultaneously, investor-driven housing construction has long characterized urban development. Over the years, large private companies have come to control most of the land available for building. As well as offering an integrated building process based on vertical links between building material production and the construction industry, these companies have weakened municipal power, promoted their own brand of development, and also managed to set the prices (Blackwell & Bengtsson 2021). In many ways this situation is a Gordian knot.

Underlying mechanisms

Housing is not an institutionally isolated sphere. On the contrary, it is a complex of production, distribution, and consumption. It is often discussed as a topic closely related to the political domain, with changes to the housing system thus framed as the result of policy changes alone, yet housing is also inextricably linked to the ever-changing framework of finance. In this dual landscape of housing-as-policy versus housing-as-market, we may find some of the explanation for the current Swedish housing crisis. According to Blackwell, scholars often relate the cause of the current housing discontent to the neoliberal turn of the 1990s. He argues that while this may be correct on an overall macro level, a more complex and multifaceted picture emerges if we consider how financing, subsidies, house prices, and building production shape micro- and meso-level urban and regional development outcomes below the level of the state (2021). This picture reveals that for at least two decades before the neoliberal turn, various tensions and contradictions in Sweden's complex of housing production, distribution, and finance led to a striking deterioration in its once highly praised housing model. There were several key factors at play, in combination: (a) inflation, leading to speculation; (b) mortgage-interest tax deductions, which allowed households to borrow money at negative interest rates, thus undermining a complex subsidy system and also leading to speculation; (c) the subsidy system itself, which encouraged the overproduction of rental housing, thereby weakening the financial position of the MHCs; and (d) the concentration of the building industry, which gained increasing power over municipal authorities. A list of circumstances that has traditionally been described as "post-1990s banking crisis phenomena" – speculation on inner-city rental housing stock, the displacement of tenants through renovations and rent hikes, the sale of public housing, soaring house prices and rent inflation, burgeoning household debt, the privatization of planning, and the deregulation of the housing finance sectors – took place throughout the 1970s and 1980s. All these changes and inherently contradictory developments led to the deterioration of the Swedish housing model and partly explain the process of neoliberalism.

Current concerns

Today the situation in Sweden, as well as in the other Nordic countries, has been exacerbated by precarious new working conditions and by the influx of foreign investment capital, which is driving up housing prices on the private market and thereby indirectly pushing up the costs of building social housing. Obviously, the means used to alleviate this situation previously cannot be brought into play again: The basic premises have changed substantially, as politics, ideology, and the economy all develop in parallel. Current planning discussions regarding what, where, and for whom we build point in several directions that are also interrelated. One trajectory concerns how to plan for diversity; another concerns how to provide affordable housing; a third concerns sustainability; and the fourth and final trajectory concerns how to understand and plan for existing social housing estates as heritage.

In the twentieth century, segregation operated on two levels. The first level enclaved housing districts into islands amid a green ocean, enforced by the hierarchical infrastructure; the second singled out each enclave by keeping apart not only the various housing types, but also the various forms of ownership and tenancy. Today, the "mixed city" has become the answer to this situation. Until recently, this meant a mixture of housing and other relevant activities. Today, the social dimension has attracted attention, in terms of having different social classes living in close proximity to one another. However, this dimension is not much debated when it comes to wealthier areas. Instead, the discussion only addresses areas with low social status, where the key question is how to attract citizens with more social capital (see Chapter 6). Yet diversity also poses a fundamental challenge to the universality of welfare states. In the planners' eagerness to balance justice and equity, the issue of diversity can easily be overlooked. On both individual and structural levels, all people have different interests and life expectations. The demographic profile of the Nordic countries has changed immensely over recent decades, taking us beyond the idea of the standard "nuclear" family comprising two opposite-sex adults and two children. According to Statistics Denmark, there are now 37 legally acknowledged types of family, and the number of singles has greatly increased. Large numbers of single-income households intensify the need for affordable housing. Moreover, the wide variety of family types entails various dynamics. Notably, some children of divorced families shuttle weekly between their parents, which means that the parents have shifting housing needs. Another dynamic revolves around a young adult's limited years of higher education, a factor that determines their housing needs during and after their time as students. This demographic diversity is further expanded by questions of cultural diversity – how we may all live together, and how the spatial framework can sustain us as we do so, both at the level of single homes and in housing clusters and districts.

Rising housing prices increasingly affect the way cities work, clustering low-income groups together and preventing younger families from putting down roots there. Rather than focusing on what kind of housing we might want, the discussion tends to focus on how far we can lower its quality: How little space is needed? How little daylight and how much noise can (young) residents tolerate, and for how long? The current move towards densification appears paradoxical in light of the enormous post-war housing efforts to provide airy, spacious living environments. But there are no easy answers as to how societies can provide affordable housing. The problems stem partly from the unavailability of resources for constructing housing in the first place, and partly from the increasing redistribution of wealth and incomes over the past four to five decades, combined with the shrinking of the middle class. The share of income going to lower-middle-income and lower-income groups is diminishing. In the US, for instance, "the share of American adults who live in middle-income households has decreased from 61% in 1971 to 51% in 2019" (Horiwitz et al. 2020). This means that the demand for affordable housing is rising. However, in growing cities there is actually no shortage of rental housing; the problem is that increasingly large numbers of people lack the incomes to afford market rents. Moreover, as municipalities compete among themselves to attract affluent citizens, they are happy to build for financially stronger population segments, while not being particularly motivated to ensure housing for financially weaker segments.

Respecting modern daily living in prefabricated buildings
The Swedish architectural firm Spridd won the Nordic Built Program competition to restore the Fittja "People's Palace" estate in Stockholm, in a transparent process that involved all stakeholders and paid attention to both the contemporary and the historical context. © John Håkansson

Environmental concerns play an increasingly important role in the building sector. While the discussion on sustainability in housing construction, in the Nordics and beyond, has long been seen as a matter of reducing energy consumption, the focus has now moved to carbon emissions. This focus is visible in the materials chosen to construct new housing. However, since substantial amounts of carbon dioxide are stored in the existing building stock, and since we have already built on most of the surface area we will need for a long time to come, attention must now be paid to the maintenance and development of existing constructions. Legal and financial incentives are needed here, although favoring retention over demolition may also have an impact on both diversity concerns and affordability.

The legacy of the Million Program in Sweden can be addressed by means other than renewal and change.

This was demonstrated in 2013 by the small architecture firm Spridd, which won the Nordic Built Cities Challenge, a competition to find new solutions for the sustainable renewal of the social housing stock (Arrhenius 2020). For their challenge, Spridd chose Fittja, a worn-down 1970s social housing suburb situated on the fringes of Stockholm, which had been part of the Million Program. Rather than the usual heavy-handed transformation, they employed conservation strategies as part of the renewal scheme. Fittja may seem an unlikely first choice for conservation: Its appearance is bland and anonymous, and the estate has no outstanding historical or other value. Indeed, like other large-scale estates from the same period, Fittja has been accused of lacking architectural quality and perpetrating social segregation. Fortunately, however, the competition rubric did not permit the sort of total reconfiguration or identity change that tends to be sought in more radical "turnaround" transformations. The architects instead offered a certain resistance to the normal procedure of contrasting "old concrete" with new materials and elements. Adopting a curatorial approach, they identified and preserved the estate's spatial and programmatic values, highlighting a number of welfare state housing qualities without suggesting radical changes. In this way, and with the addition of participatory workshops, they sought to change both the tenants' and the public's perception of Fittja as a desirable place to live.

The Swedish housing crisis is by no means an isolated crisis. It is not confined to housing – it is also a social crisis, an economic crisis, and an urban crisis. Nor is it confined to Sweden. The same problems occur elswhere with various emphases and effects.

In the next chapter, I will focus on the ongoing transformations of Danish social housing estates, addressing all of the major concerns and the multiple crisis dimensions treated in this chapter.

Chapter 6.

Transforming Danish large-scale social housing estates

Danish social housing is currently undergoing a radical transformation, with housing estates becoming mixed urban districts. Almost 30% of Denmark's current social housing stock – which houses 17–20% of the total Danish population – was built between 1959 and 1974, when the oil crisis struck. This equaled approximately one third of all housing constructed during this period; in 1966, the other two thirds of all new builds were single-family houses. The majority of mass housing going up during this period was constructed from prefabricated concrete panels, due to a special building regulation devised by the Danish government in 1960 called "the assembling regulation" (*Montagecirkulæret*). In practical terms, this regulation made financing conditional on the use of prefabricated concrete slabs; in economic terms, it kickstarted the industrialized building sector and sped up housing provision. This double bind was manifested in large-scale projects in the

country's major cities, examples being Høje Gladsaxe (in Copenhagen), Vollsmose (in Odense), and Gellerupplanen (in Aarhus).

A local response to generic challenges

When Gellerupplanen was first built, the housing estate's two sub-complexes, called Gellerup and Toveshøj, encompassed roughly 2,400 apartments in more than 30 concrete blocks of four to eight stories, covering a total of approximately 200,000 built square meters. The estate is situated in Aarhus, Denmark's second-largest city, which has about 300,000 inhabitants, and Gellerupplanen covers some 75 hectares, equaling the entire city center of Aarhus – which indicates the Gellerup estate's enormous dimensions. The period's many housing estates materialized shifting ideas about domesticity, urbanity, communal-

From local
common space to
public space
The radical physical
transformation of
the earliest Danish
"ghetto plan" estate,
Gellerup, includes
a remolding of
the landscape. It
is being reshaped
from a terraced
landscape, which
served as a
common space
for the tenants,
to a naturalistic,
undulating
landscape aimed
for use by the
public at large.
© Ellen Braae

ity, and public space in the city, and they can therefore be studied as laboratories for a broad range of ideas about "the good life" and "the good city". Dwellings, directly related functions, and a diverse range of cultural programs and features – schools, kindergartens, churches, libraries, community centers, a shopping mall, restaurants, colleges, sports and indoor swimming facilities, and numerous outdoor spaces including soccer pitches, playgrounds, and a toboggan run – were all encompassed in the large-scale plans.

Despite its architectural significance, having been designed by the architects Knud Blach Petersen and Mogens Harbo, Gellerupplanen was contested right from the start. In 1970, a couple of years before its completion, it was chosen as "Denmark's prettiest town" by the tabloid *B.T.* That same year, however, Poul Erik Skriver, the editor-in-chief of Denmark's leading architectural journal, described the development as "rationally determined" and offering only "quantitative qualities". As was also the case for similar concrete estates, the public increasingly came to regard Gellerupplanen as *samspilsramt* ("adversely impacted by multiple factors"), as explicitly stated in the 1986 Winther Report (Høghøj 2020) – a term normally used to characterize the situation of children living in dysfunctional families. Like many social housing estates from the 1960s and 1970s, Gellerup and Toveshøj were intended to accommodate urban migration and provide homes for the growing numbers of workers in new industries. Instead, however, they became residential areas for the social classes most urgently in need of housing, not least the immigrants originally known as "guest workers".[6] These immigrants began arriving in Denmark shortly after many of these estates were built, and they were assigned housing there by the municipal authorities.

In 2011, a collaboration between the municipality of Aarhus and the local Brabrand Housing Association ini-

6. Many workers came to Denmark – especially from Turkey – encouraged by the Danish government on behalf of the country's rapidly expanding industrial sector, which was in serious need of labor

tiated the transformation of Gellerup and Toveshøj – the largest renewal of any Danish social housing estate to that date. They conducted the project in collaboration with the National Building Foundation, which funds the maintenance and renovation of social housing estates across the country, with contributions from the rent paid by all of Denmark's social housing estate tenants. The decision was based on a master plan to transform Gellerupplanen from a "vulnerable [udsat] residential area into an attractive district with a flourishing urban life, a diverse resident base, a safe environment, and stimulating architecture." This was to happen by means of "radical physical change" (Aarhus Kommune & Brabrand Boligforening 2011: 5). Much like the word samspilsramt, the concept of a "vulnerable" estate indicates fragility because of exposure to various challenges. The overall aim of the transformation was very similar to the ambition embedded in the initial plans: to provide a setting for the good life. But there were also differences. At this point, the good life had come to be associated with an urban setting, and the area originally designated for residential use was changed into an urban district, and thereby indirectly given a multifunctional repurposing. Moreover, the notion of "stimulating architecture" was more subjective, and it directly addressed critiques of concrete in general and the repetitious nature of prefab architecture in particular. It could also be seen as a distancing from the ideal of equality that had been such an integral value in the social housing estates built in the 1960s and 1970s.

The initial master plan of 2007 rested on principles dealing directly and radically with the physical layout of the Gellerup and Toveshøj sub-complexes. First, the infrastructure was transformed from the original cul-de-sac roads into a combination of a transecting "urban road" running through the area's "green heart" – connecting Bazar Vest and City Vest, the two major shopping destinations used by local people and also by visiting shoppers – with a fully circular road (known as "the loop") and side roads connecting this infrastructural "island" to its wider urban context. Second, the green heart was narrowed into a long stream-like stretch linking it to two larger green networks. Consequently, new networks and subdistricts were expected to emerge and to sustain a stronger, down-scaled local identity and sense of belonging among the inhabitants of these subcommunities (Aarhus Kommune & Brabrand Boligforening 2011: 9). The 2007 principles were discussed and put to a vote among the tenants of Gellerup and Toveshøj, and the rather abstract principles were adopted. This was followed by an architecture competition and the merging of the two winning plans into the Disposition Plan. This plan was then adopted by the city council of Aarhus and confirmed by Brabrand Housing Association in 2011.

Following the main principles described above, the plan's main feature was a new road named Karen Blixen Boulevard,[7] which resembled a Parisian boulevard and had multiple lanes for cars, buses, pedestrians, cyclists, and potentially a light railway in the future. Three building blocks had to be demolished to make room for it, another two had to be altered, and one was sold off for non-residential purposes. A "golden gate" was later added to the plan, breaking through one of the eight-story housing blocks with a six-story gateway to accommodate a road linking the estate area to an adjacent high-income suburb. The green heart – now re-labeled an "urban park" – was also rejuvenated with special features intended to appeal to young people, including a large all-weather soccer pitch and multipurpose playing fields alongside the existing indoor swimming facilities. The landscape design of the new urban park undulates and unifies all the former terrain areas into a soft relief, making room for storm water and diversifying the vegetation profile. Moreover, the plan for-

7. Named after the famous aristocratic Danish author Karen Blixen (1885-1962)

71

mulated new programming, specifying new functions for new buildings, while also introducing new building types. This was followed by numerous architecture competitions for the urban park, the inclusion of various new buildings, and the redevelopment of key locations on the estate.

The governmental transformation plan

In 2018, the Danish government launched another package of initiatives meant to address the areas regarded as "ghettos" (see note 2 on page 15). Entitled *One Denmark without parallel societies: No ghettos in 2030* (*Ét Danmark uden parallelsamfund: Ingen ghettoer i 2030*) (Regeringen 2018b), this package was more radical than its predecessors. The first of the package's 22 initiatives point to physical changes, including the demolition of housing blocks, which would pave the way for sweeping new plans to alter the profile of local residents and create permanent change – making room to "start over". By selling property, demolishing buildings, and fundamentally transforming the area's physical appearance, the aim was to provide the basis for developing "a new and more attractive urban district integrated with the rest of society" (Regeringen 2018b).

This approach rested on particular definitions, setting up a four-stage logic of categories ranging from "social housing area" through "vulnerable area" to "ghetto" (later re-labeled as "parallel society") and "hard ghetto". In the first outline, a "vulnerable area" was defined as a physically coherent social housing area that had a minimum of 1,000 citizens and met at least two of five criteria: (1) a certain proportion of immigrants and people of non-Western descent; (2) a certain proportion of adult citizens who were out of work and not in education; (3) a specified level of crime; (4) a certain proportion of residents with low levels of education; and (5) average income compared with the regional average. The task defined for the last category, the "hard ghettos" (subsequently re-labeled "transformation areas"), is to reduce the share of social housing from 100% to 40%. This means reducing the part formerly owned by the social housing association by 60%. In 2019, a new "prevention" category was added, inserting another step before a social housing area is designated "vulnerable". In Denmark, as of 2021, there were 62 social housing areas categorized as prevention areas, 20 as vulnerable areas, 12 as parallel societies, and 17 as transformation areas.

The Gellerup-informed Ghetto Plan

When Gellerupplanen was put in the "hard ghetto" category in 2018, it had already long been addressing some of its major challenges, thanks to the plans from 2007 and 2011 – so little changed as a result of this latest initiative. In addition to its social problems and crime-related challenges – approximately 50% of residents were outside the labor market, 3–4.5% had criminal records, the educational level was 15–20% below the Danish average, and the average income level was slightly below the region's – Gellerupplanen was often described as different from its surrounding context, partly adding to its stigmatization. This was furthered by it being perceived as an isolated pocket in the wider urban fabric, in combination with its high concentration of "vulnerable" citizens. Its scale was also seen as a challenge, both internally and externally, which contributed to its otherwise high-quality architecture being regarded as boring and monotonous – a feature amplified by the unvarying form of ownership (the housing association). Finally, it was thought of as monofunctional, although in fact this perception did not reveal the whole story. As noted earlier, the dwellings were supported by an extremely diverse range of facilities and amenities designed for a leisure society.

The 2011 Disposition Plan (Aarhus Kommune & Brabrand Boligforening 2011) had aimed to mitigate these challenges by means of a new infrastructure, new functions, a change of institutions, new attractions, new forms of ownership, demolition, and building renovation. Indeed, the national Ghetto Plan itself was informed by the Gellerupplanen initiatives. Therefore, when Gellerupplanen became subject to that very Ghetto Plan, it could simply adjust and specify the existing plans in order to achieve the required reduction to 40% social housing apartments. This entailed the demolition of an additional 600 apartments, and the erection of 903 private housing units and of business premises equivalent to 231 units. Interestingly, Brabrand Housing Association had planned to add the non-social housing units within the existing fabric of social housing. However, Aarhus municipality preferred to achieve a social mix by creating new subdistricts, each characterized by one form of ownership, in the area outside "the golden gate".

No mixed city with the Ghetto Plan

Ostensibly, the national Ghetto Plan will create mixed cities in Denmark, which (as we saw in Chapter 5 on the Swedish housing crisis) is a valid goal. However, the Ghetto Plan may not be the proper means to achieve this. Working with two colleagues,[8] I have offered several reasons why it will not achieve its goal (Braae et al. 2020). It is definitely important to increase the level of contact between social groups. Doing so would make social housing estates more visible and strengthen their connection to the surrounding city, and such a development is currently being supported by the reconfiguration of the relevant school districts to counteract social segregation. Even so, the demolition of many social housing apartments is happening at a time when the need for affordable housing is critical, and increasing. New social housing *is* being built, but it is not affordable, due to the high costs of land and construction.

8. These colleagues – Deane Simpson from the Danish Royal Academy, and Tom Nielsen from the Aarhus School of Architecture – are both professors of urban planning. We co-authored an article that appeared in the Danish daily newspaper *Information*

The Ghetto Plan prescribes the relocation of up to 60% of tenants. A 2021 estimate indicated that 11,000 will have to leave their homes, and another 5,500 will need to be rehoused during the renovation work (Reiermann & Andersen 2019). Those who cannot be rehoused on the same estate will have to move elsewhere, most likely creating similar challenges in their new locations. They will probably go to areas and cities with less-than-ideal conditions to accommodate their needs for education, jobs, and so on. This is seen as necessary, but it contradicts research findings and practices that have revealed positive aspects of social networks within housing areas, which can help to combat poverty and crime, and which stimulate integration.

The Ghetto Plan will put tenant democracy – a key aspect of the Danish social housing model – on hold. This positions the estate itself as an authoritarian system, causing a feeling of powerlessness among residents – a feeling that has been seen to manifest violently elsewhere in Europe. In general, the social housing sector is being weakened by the Ghetto Plan, even while the sector has a crucial role to play in mitigating the neoliberal housing market and its segregationist tendencies. By international standards, Danish cities are socially well balanced, highly mixed, and attractive, and in our view the Danish housing associations and their model of organization is a key factor in this. The consequence of a weakened social housing sector is that the supply of affordable housing is heavily reduced. It is not possible to increase the number of affordable homes in the larger cities, since it is not possible to build affordable housing without additional economic support – so we can only work with what is already available.

My colleagues and I have also addressed the speed of the physical changes taking place; many mistakes will happen given the massive scale of the transformation plans. Such mistakes could be remedied by a more grad-

ual process that would allow learnings to be integrated over time. Take Gellerup as an example: The first ambitious plan was adopted in 2007, but despite massive public and private investment it is still less than halfway to achieving its goal of creating a mixed city. Whatever the scale of the economic costs might be (and at the time of writing, no financial overview for the Gellerup transformation is available), those costs may be multiplied by the number of other transformation areas, and the ultimate effects remain unknown. In the words of the respected Danish media house and thinktank Mandag Morgen, "the plan could rightly be called the greatest social experiment of this century" (Reiermann & Andersen 2019).

The mixed city is not the only important question to be considered when discussing the future of social housing estates. There is also the matter of their status as twentieth-century heritage. This matter has received no atten-

The spatial logic
of the functionally
segregated post-war
city

The two categories
of post-war
housing – the
detached single-
family houses
and the large-
scale multi-story
housing estates (of
which Tingbjerg,
shown here, is an
example) – are
both organized as
mono-functional
enclaves separated
by green areas
and infrastructure.
© Helene Høyer
Mikkelsen

tion at all in the context of Gellerupplanen, although it has been part of the discussion of plans for the heavy densification of the Tingbjerg estate. On the one hand, heritage can be understood in the traditional sense as objects that should be preserved for the future. On the other, it can be seen as a process that is not only about the past, but also about "caring for the future" (Harrison 2015). In this light, heritage-making – designating an area or structure as heritage by inquiring how people can reevaluate its spatial frameworks and explore their future roles – can be seen as an activity that holds an enormous potential for sustaining meaningful living environments, with huge positive social and environmental impacts as a result.

velopment in a straightforward way as development that met the needs of the present without compromising the ability of future generations to meet their own needs. After a period of unlimited growth, the report argued, greed and the race for profit were now the main causes of the world's unsustainable development. Nonetheless, there was an open question about how to interpret the concept of sustainability in practical planning and policy-making. The answers initially headed in two different directions. One pointed towards the eco-village model: small, self-sufficient settlements that would provide a spatial framework for food cultivation, circular production, reuse, sharing, and consumption in general. The other trajectory was the compact city, the model advocated by the 1990 European Union Green Paper on the environment. The compact city's main achievements would be energy and land efficiency, reduction of carbon emissions, and "urban qualities". Land efficiency would be achieved through the densification of already urbanized areas, thereby increasing the use of existing infrastructures and avoiding greenfield development. This would help to preserve biodiversity and spare farmland; in addition, it would shorten distances and thus reduce carbon emissions thanks to collective transportation and reduced traffic. The idea was that the compact city would facilitate travel on foot, by bicycle, and by public transportation. The drive for energy efficiency favored building types such as multi-family dwellings, as these use less energy than single-family houses and are usually smaller in size. Lastly, this model would deliver "urban qualities", as opposed to the qualities (or lack of qualities) associated with urban sprawl (Næss 2020).

In parallel with the politicians' adoption of the compact city model, a discussion was taking place among academics. The key question was whether continued economic growth was compatible with sustainable development, as the compact city model promised. One camp answered

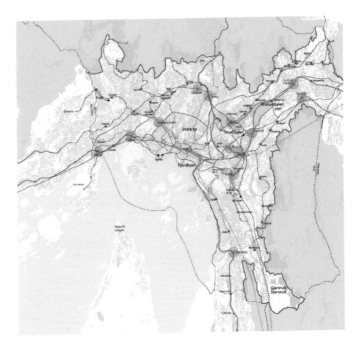

The geographical limitation of the city of Oslo
Nestled between fjord and forested mountains, Oslo has decided to densify. © Oslo kommune – Plan- og bygningsetaten

"yes" and called for ecological modernization. The other camp rejected this view, stating that sustainable development would only be possible with "de-growth". However, the vague definition of the compact city, and the consequently vague measurements, make it difficult to operationalize. Moreover, there are other goals associated with the compact city that are not dependent on density, as my discussion of access to green open spaces will demonstrate in a moment. Density can come about in many ways and on many scales, heavily affecting the context in which it occurs. This can undoubtedly impact quality of life, raising questions about whether the compact city is a desirable place to live.

The compact city in practice

In 1992–1993, the compact city became Norwegian national policy. National policy guidelines now give priority to integrated land use and transport planning, and to compact cities and densification. A White Paper on sustainable development points to public transport as the number one issue, followed by urban centers as hubs for workplaces, dwellings, shops, and cultural facilities. It also stresses the importance of protecting green infrastructure and large natural areas. As several researchers have stated, while none of these aspects are new to urban planning, they are all brought together here in the idea of the compact city.

Oslo is situated in southern Norway at the bottom of a long, large fjord, where several streams from the hinterland meet the sea. The fabric of the city is mainly located along the shore, as the forested mountain range of Marka delimits urban development to the west, north, and east. Although Oslo already covers areas on both sides of the fjord (including Sandvika and Asker on the western side, and Ski and Ås on the eastern side), as well as a broad urbanized finger reaching east towards Lillestrøm, the densified areas are particularly located in the inner city. The urban area is shaped like an inverted "U", or a lower-case "n", molded around the body of water and surrounded by a large n-shape of natural landscape. Put simply, it is the dot in the inner part of the fjord that has been designated for densification.

In planning practice, the compact city has coincided with a neoliberal turn. The 2015 Municipal Plan for Oslo clearly incorporated a growth ideology, stressing its role in the global competition for business establishments and investments, and subsequently a need to boost innovation, creativity, and organizational energy (Falleth & Saglie 2016). Moreover, market-oriented planning coincided with the advent of new public management, which strives for administrative efficiency and economic freedom, seeking liberation from political control.

Planning is now mainly driven by private initiatives and is no longer an exclusively public activity. Private developers favor density too, but from a slightly different perspective. For them, higher density equals higher profit. In Norway, private actors can submit their development ideas for political approval, a role taken on by the municipalities. The developer is responsible for the planning process, while the municipal planning authorities guide the planning proposals. To be more precise, the developer is responsible for plan-making, participation, and public information, while the planning authority is responsible for conducting formal public hearings and receiving political approval. Moreover, this planning system allows for the adoption of development plans that may not be in accordance with higher-level plans. This "planning by projects" approach risks reducing both democratic transparency and political planning accountability, and it is clear that the protection of green areas it provides is weak. Like affordable housing – we cannot get any more than we already have, due to today's high construction costs and land prices – green space, too, is a limited resource.

Achievements and limitations

Oslo has definitely managed to become denser. The number of persons per hectare of urbanized land in Oslo has increased, from a low point of 25 in 1985 to almost 40 around 2020. The urban containment policies of Oslo and other Norwegian cities have saved land and reduced the amount of car travel.

However, the costs and carbon emissions related to the construction of new housing, business, and infrastructure are not included in the calculated achievements of the new system. As the Norwegian planning professor Petter Næss importantly states, densification in itself is not a sufficient means of obtaining urban sustainability (2020). The primary purpose of building and other con-

83

struction work is not to protect the environment, but to improve the material standard of living and stimulate economic growth. Even when environmentally sound building methods are used, they are only sound compared with other, more harmful solutions. Næss goes even further, outlining the limits to the densification strategy at the core of the compact city. Firstly, the opportunities for densification – especially the most environmentally friendly opportunities – will gradually be exhausted. Secondly, much densification happens in post-industrial areas, which are themselves a limited resource; moreover, many of the former industries will occupy new land elsewhere, thereby indirectly counteracting the land savings achieved. Thirdly, the environmental load will inevitably increase, as merely seeking to sustain current levels will lead to increased environmental degradation. Fourthly, if the growth of the total building stock is to be curbed as part of the densification strategy, this will lead to the demolition of the most environmentally problematic parts of the building stock – which store large quantities of carbon dioxide. Further, although recycling is a prized strategy, it is by no means an environmentally neutral one, as the very process of recycling consumes energy and material resources.

As the densification process begins to imitate the post-war city's centrifugal growth, the need to transform the infrastructure is gaining attention. The Oslo traffic artery Østre Aker Vei is currently seen as a barrier to mixed-use development in the ring around the inner city. A typical case in point, in the 1960s and 1970s this formerly rural road was turned into an expressway to serve the largely industrial suburban corridor going northeastwards. Today, the 11-kilometer stretch must not only fulfill large-scale infrastructural purposes; it must also provide a new, aesthetically and environmentally attractive backbone with qualities that support the life of the city (Lecoart & Ming 2020).

Limited green open spaces within the dense city
The small-scale green open spaces in Oslo are under pressure. Today, large-scale structures such as the harbor front and the open areas along the Aker River serve as major recreational areas.
© Wikimedia Commons

Saving the green

As mentioned, Oslo won the 2019 European Green Capital Award, which is judged on a specific set of criteria. The Norwegian capital was highlighted for protecting the expansive natural areas around the city and for reopening a number of streams. It is a green city with parks, trees, wooded areas, and waterways, and green values have played an important role in its planning history. There are no total measurements of the green spaces lost to the densification process, although one research project found a net loss of 7.23 square meters per inhabitant in only two years, between 1994 and 1996 – equivalent to 640 soccer pitches. According to the Municipal Plan, all lost green areas are to be replaced, but this has clearly not happened. This indicates a general decline in the number and size of recreational areas, particularly in the dense city districts that might have the greatest need for them (Falleth & Saglie 2016). One national report calculated a reduction from 70 to 67 square meters per inhabitant between 1999 and 2005 (Falleth & Saglie 2016: 7).

While public agencies and private developers forge alliances in the quest for densification, researchers Eva Falleth and Inger-Lise Saglie (Stenbro et al. 2016) have concluded that "the role of advocate for the protection of the green areas is left to other actors" – that is, to residents. Local groups are fighting for their local landscapes and urban wooded areas, attempting to mediate the fragmentation of both the planning system and the green structure of the city.

Commons, or shared spaces in the local neighborhood, are often considered a more valuable resource by inhabitants than by authorities or developers. Such spaces could potentially be ascribed heritage values, yet green commons may not fit into the monumental and often material authoritative conception of cultural heritage. Indeed, such places often undergo a constant process of production and reproduction through residents' use, consumption, negotiation, and play, and as such they operate as local heritage. This is not recognized by decision-makers, however, and it does not enter the formal decision-making processes of developers and politicians. Likewise, intangible issues of spatial and place identity rarely gain a foothold when densification processes are discussed (Stenbro et al. 2016).

The post-pandemic city

The Oslo densification process has been ongoing for about three decades, and much has happened in that time. The post-war city was open, whether it comprised detached single-family houses or large-scale housing estates. The compact city model is very different, even though it is unfolding within the framework of the existing, partly post-war city. One major argument in favor of the post-war city form was that it would provide healthy and recreation-friendly surroundings. It is therefore interesting to explore how the compact city has worked as a spatial framework during the COVID-19 pandemic.

The pandemic has certainly brought about significant changes to human mobility patterns and working environments. Norwegian research on movement patterns in Oslo during the lockdown there estimated that outdoor recreational activities rose by a staggering 291%.[9] By using mobile tracking data from thousands of recreationists, it was possible to measure 86,000 additional activities across the municipality, whose population is 690,000 (Venter et al. 2020). These vast numbers cover walking, running, hiking, and cycling. Cyclists rode far and wide on trails that were easily accessible; pedestrians visited city parks, peri-urban open areas, and nature preserves. The conclusion was loud and clear: Access to green open spaces woven into the built-up matrix is very important. But these findings also reveal some dilemmas concerning green equity and justice: Who has access to which green open spaces? The denser the city is, the less green it is, too. The open spaces, as potential building spots and thus areas for profit-making, are extremely valuable and reserved for the most expensive housing.

And the findings show us more. Norwegian planning researcher Kostas Mouratidis made in-depth measurements of health and well-being before and during the pandemic (2022). He discovered that living in a higher-density neighborhood – the core of the compact city – was associated with lower life satisfaction, lower happiness, and lower leisure satisfaction during the pandemic. Residents here often live in smaller apartments, are dependent on public transport, and lack green open spaces nearby. Living in an apartment did not, in itself, contribute negatively to health and well-being during the pandemic; quite

9. Pre-pandemic, the level of outdoor activity in Norway was already relatively high, as much of the country's population outside Oslo has easy access to go hiking, skiing, etc.

the contrary. But living in smaller dwellings did reduce life satisfaction and happiness during that time, and this was related to the link between poor housing and the increased risk of depression during the pandemic. People living alone and families with children were particularly under pressure from these factors. Moreover, public transportation, which is closely related to the strengths of the compact city, turned out to have a negative influence on health and well-being, possibly due to the increased risk of infection and stress it caused. Green open spaces played a positive, counteractive role to public transportation, and also supported leisure activities.

The travel restrictions issued in the first phase of the pandemic revealed another dimension of the compact city model. This concerned the status of second homes – the many cabins (*hytter*), as they are still called today, despite their often ample size and lodge-like comfort. Norway has a long-standing tradition of going into the mountains (*på fjellet*) to stay at one's cabin (*på hytta*). The forested mountain range of Marka closely surrounds and spatially delimits Oslo. Beyond Marka lie Norway's vast and sparsely populated mountain regions. Within 200 kilometers of the center of Oslo there are some 190,000 cabins, about one third of which are owned by Oslo residents (Schnell & Skjulhaug 2020). The government's pandemic travel restrictions only allowed cabin owners to use their cabins if they were located within the same municipality as their main residence. This restriction became a topic of fierce debate in Norway. Cabin owners claimed that they would never have bought their cabins if they had known there would be any restrictions on their use, and declared that it was their human right to go and stay in their cozy *hytte*. The Home Guard was called out to ensure that people went where they were supposed to go – back to the city – and the minister for health and social affairs wrote a public letter instructing everyone to go home and stay there.

The pandemic restrictions clearly revealed the role of cabin life as a driver of urbanization processes. Normally, cabin life in Norway is associated with nature, the mountains, and rural areas, and as such it is seen as complementary to urban life. Cabins today are by no means primitive. Most are more than 100 square meters in size and meet the same technical construction requirements as primary residences in terms of water and heat supply, insulation, and so forth. The higher their standard, the more they are used. The administrative "grid" of the municipalities does not reflect this use pattern. Indeed, the most highly prized cabin areas are far removed from the major cities of Oslo and Bergen, but they are nonetheless considered part of those cities' hinterlands. Such cabins contribute to both "recreational commuting" and "recreational urban sprawl".

The Norwegian cabin debate, provoked by pandemic restrictions, revealed that cabins are part of an urbanization pattern that dismantles the distinction between urban and rural: The rural is urbanized and becomes part of the city. This pattern affects the size of a resident's home when their secondary home is included, and it affects the amount of traffic as well. It also has impacts on rural areas, reducing biodiversity and increasing urban land use and infrastructure. Overall, the cabin phenomenon is entirely in contrast with the aims that guided the compact city policy at the outset. This dual settlement pattern can be found in many places, across the Nordics and far beyond, where significant increases in housing prices allow people to invest in second homes. The seeming overlap in the interests of sustainability ideals and investor-building have a downside that potentially skews or nullifies the entire sustainability push. The scope and nature of the "double settlement" trend makes it more or less insignificant how much anyone cycles or takes the metro on a daily basis.

Chapter 8.

Climate adaptations transforming the public space

All Nordic cities are connected to the same global reality when it comes to climate change. This is true even though the changes vary geographically. The northern reaches of Europe will see higher winter temperatures, while the southern reaches will become warmer in summer, and Europe as a whole will see more frequent heavy-rain events. Adapting to these changes, mitigating them, and preventing further damage is a process that will affect cities, their public spaces, and how these spaces are used. For Denmark, with its large archipelago, its extensive coastlines, and its capital and most other major towns and cities near the sea, climate change is intimately associated with water and changing precipitation patterns. One of the most significant planning challenges for Copenhagen is to prepare the flat coastal metropolis to handle the increasing amounts of rainfall projected for the future.

The increasing number of heavy rainstorms and flooding events suddenly found its way to the top of the public agenda in Denmark, and among insurance companies, when a succession of rainwater events hit Copenhagen in 2010 and 2011. The first occurred in August 2010, leaving cellars flooded. But the real cloudburst occurred in July the following year and affected the entire city. In just ninety minutes, more than 135 mm of rain fell on the city center, with measured volumes exceeding 60 mm within one half hour. The result of this downpour on an otherwise pleasant summer day was that infrastructure, institutions, and many homes were flooded. The total insurance payouts after this unusual event, known simply as *skybruddet*, "the cloudburst", have been calculated at 4.88 billion Danish kroner (some 692 million US dollars), excluding the costs incurred by public institutions that were self-insured. After the second event the insurance companies

Climate change as heavy rain
Two large rain events within one year were a wake-up call for Copenhagen. Both events exceeded the capacity of the sewer system, flooding streets and basements, and subsequently making local politicians decide to adopt the city's radical "Cloudburst Plan". © Bax Lindhardt / Ritzau Scanpix

stated that they would not cover any costs arising from a third event unless measures were taken, and mechanisms installed, to prevent similar damage. This was the starting point for what was later dubbed the Copenhagen Cloudburst Plan, which was adopted by the city council in 2012 (City of Copenhagen 2011).

The Copenhagen Cloudburst Plan

With the Cloudburst Plan, the City of Copenhagen decided that adapting to the changing precipitation patterns would entail more than just enlarging the existing subterranean sewer and drainage system. Rather, the rainwater must also be managed "on the ground" in a "blue-green strategy". This landscape-based approach became part of the foundation of the city's climate adaptation strategies. The decision rested on the assumption that this approach would be easier and less expensive to implement, compared to enlarging the sewer system. The key element in the Copenhagen Cloudburst Plan is, therefore, to handle heavy rainfall on urban surfaces with retention basins, sluicing it through a few huge, newly installed pipes on the final stretch from the last retention basin – the five existing inner-city lakes. This approach differs from the previous one, which led all storm-drainage water into the sewer system. Nevertheless, with precipitation patterns shifting towards more and heavier rain events, the sewer systems may still get overloaded and push sewer water to the surface of the streets, parks, and squares – and into the cellars of homes, businesses, and institutions, creating a great health risk. Very simply put, the new strategy has the streets acting as delay and transport channels, which guide the water to basins and pools (mainly on the ground) that are able to contain it, sluicing some out through the pipes to the harbor and retaining the rest until the sewer system's capacity is once again available to release it at a manageable speed. The streets therefore work in tandem with the retention and receiving areas, which, logically, are only found in existing open and often green spaces, such as parks. The Cloudburst Plan emphasizes the synergies that can be achieved between storm water management, the implementation of biodiversity measures, and the promise of upgrading urban public spaces by implementing planned initiatives.

Copenhagen as a laboratory

Copenhagen is, and over the next few decades will continue to be, a large-scale urban laboratory for the climate-adapted green city of the future. The Cloudburst Plan covers the municipalities of Copenhagen and Frederiksberg – Frederiksberg being an independent local district nested within the City of Copenhagen – with a total area of some 34 square kilometers (a good 13 square miles). It is divided into eight catchment areas, which form natural "bowls" or "basins" within an otherwise virtually flat topography that gathers the rainwater into streams that flow to the sea. Four of the eight original catchment areas have been further developed, according to three master plans. These three plans account for over half of the 300 projects slated for completion to make the whole Cloudburst Plan work. As mentioned, the main idea is to handle the water in situ, "where it lands," which immediately brings the inner parts of the city into play, as Copenhagen is located directly on the seaboard. In its subsequent phases, the plan works "upstream" from the inner city. In practice, the districts built around 1900 have been targeted first, given that the perimeter of "the inner city" is defined by the five large, shallow, interconnected lakes – a relic of the erstwhile defense system around the medieval part of the city. From there, as mentioned, huge new pipes discharge the excess water into the harbor.

The climate adaptation of public space is an issue that cuts across policy boundaries and bureaucratic domains, and solutions must be developed at multiple levels, in terms of both management and decision-making. The city was therefore obliged to set up a meta-governance structure, consisting of top-down steering and bottom-up participation in co-creative processes. As a process, "co-creation" is the merging of various inputs from experts and locals, and from public and private entities, in the search for comprehensive solutions to public problems. The city administration is therefore cooperating with integrated urban renewal projects (IUR), local committees, housing associations, owners' associations, citizens' groups, businesses, and other local stakeholders to gain insight into local challenges and the residents' dreams. This sort of cooperation effort also serves as a point of exchange and decision-making on the ground (Engberg 2017). First and foremost, however, the aim is to promote innovative, specific, workable solutions.

The Cloudburst Plan is the first of its kind in the world, and it is unique in its widespread use of integrated planning and implementation of blue–green infrastructure and, to some degree, also in its participation practices. Obviously, implementing the plan is bringing substantive technological interventions throughout the city in the form of water retention basins, drainage filters, and so forth, and it is actually reworking the topography of the green open spaces. The Cloudburst Plan will greatly change everyday spaces for many Copenhageners, and it is a new and momentous challenge – getting old, unwieldy, and sometimes incompatible technical rainwater systems to meet the citizens' demands and their wishes for the city's shared public spaces. Similar plans are currently being developed by Danish engineers in New York City, while other cities, including Gothenburg and Paris, are discussing the challenges of managing their own changing precipitation patterns.

These massive interventions will allow planners to reconsider and re-design many open spaces in Copenhagen to improve conditions for today's city-dwellers. Still, the changes being made as cities prepare for heavy rainfall events should not be mistaken for purely technological matters. Rather, they concern everything from politics to economics, ecologies, social issues, and much more. Not least, they entail a complex of cultural and aesthetic questions and are linked to specific worldviews. Like other drivers of change in our cities, climate resilience plans force us to make a whole set of cultural choices, whether we discuss them explicitly or not.

Reworking districts and parks

One of the big questions is where to retain such large amounts of water in a densely built-up cityscape. A city can choose to follow the runoff logic inferred from the existing topography. Alternatively, it can look for accessible space, in the form of publicly owned, unbuilt space. The answer to the challenge of finding available space has been to look to public parks and, to a lesser extent, urban squares. Historically, parks have already been reconfigured to contain rainwater, although mostly at the scale of the park area itself. The Cloudburst Plan for Copenhagen requires the city parks, which are often quite small, to collect and retain rainwater from areas multiple times their own size. These requirements are not without consequences for the layout and the use of such parks, and they definitely also affect the planning process and its democratic aspects.

The following is a brief overview of three illustrative examples from Copenhagen, in chronological order with the first transformation first. All three climate-adapted sites are located near the inner city: the St Kjeld district in the Østerbro neighborhood; Enghavepark in Vesterbro; and Hans Tavsens Park in Nørrebro. Each had already been designated for integrated urban renewal when it was

96

designated as a key elements in the Cloudburst Plan. As a first step, the City Council IUR partnership and the City Climate Adaptation Unit decided to create an urban design laboratory to test out co-creating solutions and user-generated innovation.

In that process, the St Kjeld district was given the role of the emergent climate-resilient neighborhood, by means of an "urban nature" strategy that targeted problems of pollution, overheating, and cloudburst management, besides providing better recreational facilities. New and untested solutions, some still in the making, were proposed, and a mock-up was even produced to show the potential of this combination of rainwater management, urban greening, and technical solutions. Meanwhile, the municipality and the utility companies are negotiating how to divide the costs, as they will share the expenses. In parallel, private foundations are being approached to cover the costs of the newer and more iconic elements of the Cloudburst Project, which naturally paves the way for such elements to be implemented.

The next test site was Enghavepark, a 3.5-hectare park from the early twentieth century, canonized for its neoclassical design and now re-designed to store 28,000 cubic meters (roughly 7.4 million US gallons) of rainwater, mostly above ground. These new mitigation requirements also encompass a desire for more "urban nature" – a new but influential concept in Copenhagen's planning, which holds the promise of reconciling nature and the city. Furthermore, the climate change adaptation measures now have to be negotiated alongside two other strong agendas for Enghavepark: heritage protection and citizen involvement. Based on a 2014 design competition, with a winning proposal entitled *Common and Unique*, the park reopened in 2019. The entry was submitted to the competition by the design company *Tredje Natur* (literally "third nature"), who were also key designers on the project in the St Kjeld district. Contrary to both the competition brief and the city's urban policy, the winning proposal chose *not* to make space for handling large amounts of rainwater visible above ground, on the park's terrain, instead suggesting a vast underground tank. This will prevent the rainwater agenda from dominating the everyday use of the park, the sports field will remain in place – only turning into something else (a basin) in the event of excessive downpour – and only small visible rain-management elements have been added. Rather than spelling the water out as a threat, the park allows it to be present as a playful component in its everyday use.

The third significant cloudburst project is the winning proposal for the Nordic Built Challenges Award for Hans Tavsens Park. The design, by the company SLA, reworks the terrain of the 8.3-hectare area to accommodate 18,000 cubic meters (nearly 4.8 million US gallons) of rainwater. A rough calculation can give a clue as to the relative proportions of the park's size and the amount of water it can retain: If the full capacity of water were equally distributed over the park's ground area, it would reach a depth of 46 centimeters – just under half a meter, or about 18 inches. Even so, the proposal preserves the park's playgrounds, pathways, and, not least, many of its old trees. The result will be a distinctly undulating terrain that will not leave much room for playing ball or picnicking. Another critical part of the proposal's approach has to do with maintaining the old trees, which may not be able to survive a 100-year rain event that leaves the soil waterlogged for days.

One common denominator of these adaptation strategies is that they aim to make cities work *with* rather than *against* nature's processes, granting water and parks, and flora and fauna, a much more prominent role in the way we organize our cities. But although blue–green solutions are always regarded as positive, other aspects that might

Climate adaptation in conflict with cultural heritage
The strategy of the Copenhagen Cloudburst Plan is to handle and retain storm water in surface reservoirs like these, in Hans Tavsens Park. Another 300 scheduled projects will transform the public spaces of the inner city, although often at the expense of cultural heritage elements and existing opportunities for daily use. © SLA / Beauty and the Bit

hold value should not be overlooked. Climate adaptation tasks are new and complex for politicians, administrators, engineers, planners, and designers. To make informed decisions, they will have to test new ways of making public space decisions, then reflect on the lessons learned from the many experiments, and finally adjust our understandings and procedures accordingly.

Considering the climate adaptation of Enghavepark to accommodate 22,600 cubic meters of storm water, and Hans Tavsens Park to accommodate 18,000 cubic meters, it is clear that such adaptation and green urban development have wider implications than ecology alone. Here, I will elaborate on four aspects: livability, democracy, heritage, and aesthetics.

"Livability" is a vague concept that addresses the interests society has in making people want to live in cities. On the one hand, the point is to attract citizens and businesses in the global competitive landscape; on the other, it is to make citizens settle down in the city and spend their leisure time where they live, thereby practicing a more sustainable way of living. However, turning important recreational spaces in a densely built-up inner city into large construction sites for years is challenging, even though it is only for a limited time. Climate adaptation work will unavoidably go on for a long time, however. When it is finished, the climate-adapted Hans Tavsens Park will not offer the same recreational value as before, since the otherwise flat lawns will have been molded into a steep and heavily undulating terrain designed to retain the rainwater if and when it eventually falls in large amounts and no longer fit for recreational use.

The degree of visible transformation in Enghavepark is fairly limited, since a significant part of the retention basins were placed under ground level and therefore do not "play by the rules," in the sense that handling all storm water on the surface was a premise. Nevertheless, the planned changes, the long transformation process, and the consequent lack of access and use are all inescapable facts. Moreover, despite the need to address climate change, the decision to adopt and implement the Cloudburst Plan comes from above, which challenges the Danish planning system's participation policies and practices. How can technical solutions sustain the social and civic life of the city, and do so not just *for* citizens but also *with* engaged citizens? Whose voices will be heard, and whose values will be promoted, in the battle between various citizens' groups? A similar question could be asked of the battle between humans and other species in the city, which I briefly touched upon above, from the perspective of a loss of livability.

Cultural heritage is challenged in such circumstances, partly by the eagerness to create new and innovative climate adaptation solutions. With such a strong focus on a future sustained by technology and biodiversity, it is easy to lose sight of the city that is being transformed. Our view on what is already there a kind of scaffolding in our minds for what this space or that structure could become in the new city. Take the five lakes described above, for which suggestions have been made to rework them into rainwater-optimized wilderness areas. What would happen to the narrative about the role they played as part of the medieval fortification system, and much later as a promenade for the capital's nineteenth-century bourgeoisie? And what will happen to the narratives about the daily life and significance of the old boroughs? All these distinctions can potentially become blurred by urban nature and by new technologies. The climate-related pressure to change may wash away the important learnings recent years have brought to city communities about their heritage and history – causing us to lose a mirror that informs us about alternative ways of thinking and living, and thus about ways of enlarging our lifeworld.

Focusing on technical solutions, we tend to overlook aesthetic implications. Often, climate adaptation projects are communicated from the perspective of what they *do* rather than how they *look*: from the perspective of which specific functions the blue and green elements offer the city and its inhabitants. Yet on examining the increasing number of green and climate-adapted urban spaces, it is obvious that, to a certain degree, they all look alike. They all draw on the same idea of beauty even though they are not the result of an aesthetically motivated choice. They offer us long-stemmed grasses, color-spattered vegetation, and surfaces in curved forms that clearly signal "biodiversity and climate adaptation" – and often, the businesses implementing this work have a signature way of bringing in certain species, affecting the appearance of the future city. Considering the number of transformations of the most significant public spaces that are scheduled to happen within a limited period, a call for expressive diversity is not unreasonable. Planning and designing of this sort obliges us to pay specific attention to the unification of the public space, ensuring that it offers individual *and* common points of reference.

These questions are all urgent, due to the speed of the transformations being driven by climate change, and also due to the challenges facing the spatial legacy of the welfare city. Multiple agendas are at play simultaneously, and we are still seeking answers to whether, and how, we can help ease the pressure on the planet by spatially organizing our cities. At present, however, we are still only just beginning to find healthier ways to understand the interaction between humans and our lifeworld. Copenhagen and other climate-adaptation laboratories do offer hope that we can create better relationships between these factors, yet we must proceed with an open mind, taking a broad view of the cities' urban public spaces and their heterogeneities - while also paying attention to the new challenges related to participation, democracy, heritage, and aesthetics. We must also bear in mind that these developments are happening in a political context that aims to attract new, strong residents and investors who will be stakeholders in the city in both the short term and the long term.

Chapter 9.
Conclusions

New welfare ideas and planning challenges continue to emerge. Post-war planners and politicians used urban planning as a tool to frame and regulate the welfare state's utopia. Ideals of egalitarianism, justice, and redistribution formed the basis of post-war policies – as gathered under the headlines of "the welfare state" and "the good life" – where new public landscapes and open spaces were social arenas for societal changes and urban expansion. The embedded policies implied multiple preservation initiatives as an undercurrent, underpinning the welfare city and making up the bedrock of the welfare state. The three Scandinavian siblings – Norway, Denmark, and Sweden – all resembled progressive welfare states, guaranteeing actions, discourse, and legislation to protect heritage interests. Furthermore, heritage played a leading role in instituting a state-backed politics of progress.

Planning dynamics and welfare dynamics

Many new connotations of the word "welfare" developed during the foundational period of the 1950s, partly shifting from wealth (*velstand*) to well-being in the political appropriation of the logic of the universal welfare state model. As the previous chapters have revealed, it is a fair claim that today the pendulum has once again swung back, so that the main focus is now on wealth in a more segregated way, in the sense of attracting wealthy residents and stable investors to a city. Many changes have occurred. These changes challenge both ideas of welfare and the planning conditions for welfare services and amenities, as discussed throughout the preceding chapters.

The role of planning has also changed. As the Danish political scientist Kaj Ove Pedersen has described, the welfare state has gradually become a competitive state (2011). The gradual shift from welfare state to competitive state is reflected in the way urban development that was previously driven by the public discourse, the state, and social housing estates has subsequently been taken over by private investors. Human beings are mainly regarded as units of labor: productive, efficient, competent entities on the competitive global playing field. The idea of welfare has been adjusted and rationalized to serve this purpose. Urbanization is scattered geographically, resulting in urban landscapes that exhibit a mix of built-up spaces and interstitial spaces, rather than cities per se. These spaces form networks that complement one another in terms of function: education, research, culture, sports, aesthetics, protecting the environment. Today, the urban welfare landscape is facing several crises. It is in need of change and must therefore be seen from a new perspective. Biodiversity loss and the climate crisis can be interpreted as part of a wider democratic crisis, and vice versa. Increasing inequity, housing problems, the issue of security of supply, and the COVID-19 pandemic are among the most obvious crises of recent times.

In this book I have addressed current welfare planning by looking at challenging topics through the lens of specific cases. We have seen how the housing crises in Sweden, across the Nordic countries, and elsewhere destabilize the social contracts between the state and its inhabitants, especially regarding vulnerable groups and their urban inclusion. We have also seen how spatial segregation has been reinforced, and how younger generations have difficulty gaining a foothold on the housing market, as well as how governmentally initiated radical transformations of social housing estates are being promoted to address some of the social challenges of spatial segregation – or rather, of the clustering of the most vulnerable groups – and yet the plan entails contradictory elements. Once again, the landscape is the element that can attract people and bring them together across social and cultural class divides – just as it did in the vision for green structural development from the 1930s onwards. Once again, housing areas have become large-scale playgrounds for private developers and contracting companies.

We have seen how the market works in tandem with sustainability-related goals of densifying the city center to reduce car-dependent traffic and to relieve pressure on the natural surroundings of the city. On these terms, efforts have been successful. Even so, the quality of life in and the ecological quality of these densely built-up areas depends on the number, the size, and the qualities of the open spaces, and as the public planning system is reduced to guiding private developers in meeting the government's requirements, the crucial green component of the compact city becomes only weakly governed and is thus losing ground.

We have further seen how urban planning is also regional planning, as pointed out early on in this book, emphasizing the role of planning in taking care of the metabolism of the city. Spatial planning is also gaining ground, however. In the context of climate adaptation, it has been shown how an efficient city administration enables radical plans for addressing change, with more and heavier rain literally transforming common, historical public spaces – prompting 300 projects in Copenhagen city center alone.

This is radical in the sense that planning procedures merge bottom-up processes with significant top-down requirements for retaining large and predefined amounts of rainwater. Finally, we have heard that the funding of such transformations also relies on private foundations, which can influence the agenda.

Themes for tomorrow's welfare planning

Taking a broad view of the current challenges we face and considering the cases I have used to show how they are being addressed, a variety of even more fundamental questions begin to emerge. These questions boil down to five grand themes that today's spatial welfare planning will have to address.

The first relates to creating *good living conditions* for all citizens. In spatial terms, this goes far beyond the individual dwelling. It concerns the ways we can, and potentially could, live together; the spatial and organizational conditions that might support the ways we meet and engage in various communities and networks; the feeling of a sense of belonging; and how we look after one another and our environment. Today, the understanding of who "we" are – this common "all" expressed in the public access rights granted by the Norwegian and Swedish concept of *allemannsrett/allemansrätt* – is gradually changing. We see the negative aspects of today's broken circle of solidarity when social engineering results in the eviction of less resourceful tenants from social housing without anyone having an idea of where they can go. Basically, this demonstrates that the otherwise good idea of the mixed city has a darker side due, among other things, to its preference for the lower middle class. From a broader perspective, humanity has come to understand that the future of our own species depends not just on our own survival, but on the survival of all living organisms.

The second grand theme concerns *sustainable development*, a brand of development that meets the needs of the present without compromising the ability of future generations to meet their own needs - to quote the Brundtland Report once again. The pressure *on* nature and the role *of* nature are two interlinked issues that are becoming increasingly important. The paradox of preserving nature while continuing to give people access to it is still a main aim of spatial and urban planners, and it is taking on more diverse and complex forms given the loss of biodiversity and the reality of climate change. The recent focus on how to reduce carbon emissions has changed the game, as increasingly sophisticated calculation models are now able to include the carbon footprints of existing buildings and infrastructure, and of construction as well. Although this too may seem paradoxical, the apparently green trends of post-war urbanization - largely a result of Western industrial culture - have led to the current environmental crisis. And on top of this, tomorrow's sustainable cities must be fashioned on and around the relatively flawed cities we have today.

The third grand theme addresses *heritage*, taking up another consequence of the fact that an overwhelming share of the total built-up space and urban areas originated in the post-war period. There is a pressing need to address this legacy in more inclusive ways than is currently the case. Rather than being taken seriously as a genuine object of heritage, post-war architectural production is more often subject to the privatization of land or assimilation policies, new urban agendas, urban renewal, and renovation projects. Official heritage policies, if they address the "young" legacy of the post-war period at all, often restrict their interest to a few selected buildings and sites. Gradually, however, they are beginning to receive more interest. For one thing, the interest in heritage has been growing, and for another, many structures from this period have passed the age of 50, which is the official threshold in Denmark for considering potential heritage objects. Besides noting the vast amounts of carbon embedded in older buildings, there is an increasing acknowledgement of their value to local residents. On a more general level, heritage is a grand theme for planning because there is a dynamic tension that arises when planners discuss what is *already there* and ideas for how it might find new uses and guises in the future.

The fourth grand theme follows directly from the third; it has to do with *dialogue and participation* and the tensions and diverging views between experts and laymen, and between the private and the public spheres. Democratic processes are challenged by urban development logics, spatial segregation, and the top-down climate adaptation decisions being made, as described in cases from Sweden, Norway, and Denmark. However, it is still a basic requirement in each and every case to conduct an open, honest dialogue between the public administrators and the community to maintain the high level of trust in the authorities and to ensure local engagement. One important goal of such dialogue is finding support for innovative solutions in the messy plurality of public and private ideas, justifications, and knowledge – all governed as a top-down management process of bottom-up participation in co-creative processes.

This leads us to the fifth and final grand theme, which relates to the coherence of society and concerns *social and spatial justice*. The challenging topics discussed in this book's main chapters can be addressed in various ways, yet they need to be resolved in ways that are socially and spatially equitable and just. This is also a key theme for the welfare planning of today and tomorrow. The formal *and* informal planning of cross-sectorial and bureaucratic cross-boundary areas calls for multiple levels of information and dialogue within the planning administration itself

– both vertically, in the sense that various decision levels must be mutually coordinated, and horizontally, in the sense that various fields of knowledge should be activated. Public-private co-creation processes emphasize the need for dialogue that is guided by the planning administration but transcends individual stakeholders. To stimulate such co-creation, the public administration should engage in constructive collaboration with relevant actors to define and share problems and manage collective tasks. Obviously, however, this is more easily said than done in light of the enormity of some of the challenges we face.

To borrow a headline from the Sustainable Development Goals of the United Nations, which could easily have been brought into play in this book but would have swelled its scope, the guide to future development is "leave no one behind." Socially just decisions are also spatially just, and they concern everyone's welfare – the "we" and the "all". In this sense urban planning, and in fact all spatial planning, remains a powerful tool that brings the concept of welfare back to center stage, both in the Nordics and beyond.

Suggestions for further reading

Braae, E., Riesto, S., Steiner, H., & Tietjen, A. (Eds.). (2021). Special Issue on Welfare Landscapes. *Landscape Research*, *44*(4).

Christiansen, C., Bro, P. H., Damgaard, L., Hollesen, D., Monfared, L., Skjøt-Pedersen, J., Tønsberg, H. V., & Wiil, A.-S. (Eds.). (2016). *Den Grønne Metropol*. Frydenlund Academic.

Gudmand-Høyer, S., Bach, R. C., Jensen, B. G., Moseng, K., Nielsen, T., Olesen, K., & Vestergaard, I. (2021). *Gellerup*. The Danish Architectural Press.

Lotz, K., Simpson, D., Raahauge, K. M., Vindum, K., Jensen, M. J., & Bendsen, J. R. (Eds.). (2017). *Forming Welfare*. The Danish Architectural Press.

Swenarton, M., Avermaete, T., & van den Heuvel, D. (Eds.). (2014). *Architecture and the Welfare State*. Routledge.

References

Albertsen, N. & Diken, B. (2013). Welfare and the City. *Nordisk Arkitekturforskning*, *17*(2), 257-275.

Arrhenius, T. (2020). Restoring the Public: The Case of Fittja Suburb. In S. Riesto & M. Glendinning (Eds.), *Mass Housing of The Scandinavian Welfare States: Exploring Histories and Design Approaches*. 39-44. University of Edinburgh.

Bech-Danielsen, C., Mechlenborg, M., & Stender, M. (2018). *Welcome Home: Trends in Danish Housing Architecture*. Politikens Forlag.

Blackwell, T. (2021). Power, production and disorder: The decline of Sweden's housing industrial complex and the origins of the present housing discontents. *European*

Urban and Regional Studies, 28(4), 338–352. https://doi.
org/10.1177/09697764211009570

Blackwell, T. & Bengtsson, B. (2021). The resilience of social
rental housing in the United Kingdom, Sweden and
Denmark. How institutions matter. *Housing Studies.*
https://doi.org/10.1080/02673037.2021.1879996

Bro, H. (2016). Hovedstadsmetropolen og Den grønne
betænkning. In C. Christiansen et al. (Eds.), *Den
Grønne Metropol. Natur og recreative områder i
hovedstadsmetropolen efter 1900.* 155–194. HOKA.

Braae, E. (2017). Welfare Landscapes and Communities. In
K. Lotz et al. (Eds.), *Forming Welfare.* 34–49. Danish
Architectural Press.

Braae, E. (2020). Non-Site Welfare Landscapes On-Site: Curated
Displays of Transformed Social Housing Estates.
Landscape Research 1–16. https://doi.org/10.1080/0142639
7.2020.1808955

Braae, E. (2021). Naturen og byen. *Arkitekten, 08,* 42–51.

Braae, E., Nielsen, T., & Simpson, D. (2020, November 14). Her
er fem grunde til, at ghettoloven ikke er løsningen på at
skabe en blandet by. *Information.*

Braae, E., Riesto, S., Steiner, H., & Tietjen, A. (2020). Welfare
Landscapes. Open Spaces of Danish Social Housing
Estates. In M. Glendinning & S. Riesto (Eds.), *Mass
Housing of the Scandinavian Welfare States: Exploring
Histori es and Design Strategies.* 13–23. University of
Edinburgh.

Braae, E. & Steiner, H. (2021). Expanding Danish Welfare
Landscapes – Steen Eiler Rasmussen and Tingbjerg
Housing Estate. In J. Haffner (Ed.), *The Environment
Built: Dwelling as Landscape in Twentieth-Century
Urbanism.* 146–167. Routledge.

City of Copenhagen. (2011). *Cloudburst Management Plan 2012.*
The City of Copenhagen. Technical and Environmental
Administration.

CRUSH. (2016). *Tretton myter om bostadsfrågan.* Dokument Press.

Cullen, G. (1977). *The Concise Townscape.* The Architectural Press.

Engberg, L. (2017). Climate Adaptation and Citizens' Participation in Denmark: Experiences from Copenhagen. In S. Hughes, E. K. Chu., & S. G. Mason (Eds.), *Climate change in cities: Innovations in multi-level governance.* 139-161. Springer International Publishing AG. https://doi.org/10.1007/978-3-319-65003-6_8

Esping-Andersen, G. (1990). *Three Worlds of Welfare Capitalism.* Blackwell Press.

Falleth, E. & Saglie, I.-L. (2016). Planning a Compact Oslo. In P. G. Røe & M. Luccarelli, *Green Oslo. Visions. Planning and Discourse.* 257-272. Routledge.

Gudmand-Høyer, S., Bach, R. C., Jensen, B. G., Moseng, K., Nielsen, T., Olesen, K., & Vestergaard, I. (2021). *Gellerup.* The Danish Architectural Press.

Gutman, M. & de Coninck-Smith, N. (2008). *Designing Modern Childhoods: History, Space, and the Material Culture of Children.* Rutgers University Press.

Harrison, R. (2015). Beyond "Natural" and "Cultural" Heritage: Toward an Ontological Politics of Heritage in the Age of Anthropocene. *Heritage & Society, 8*(1), 24-42.

Horowiz, J. M., Igielnik, R., & Kochhar, R. (2020). *Most Americans Say There Is Too Much Economic Inequality in the U.S., but Fewer Than Half Call it a Top Priority.* Pew Research Center.

Høghøj, M. (2020). Mass Housing and the Emergence of the 'Concrete Slum' in Denmark in the 1970s & 1980s. In S. Riesto & M. Glendinning (Eds.), *Mass Housing of the Scandinavian Welfare States.* 8-18. University of Edinburgh.

Judt, T. (2005). *Postwar. A History of Europe since 1945.* Penguin Books.

Jørgensen, K. & Thorén, K. H. (2016). Planning for a Green Oslo. In P. G. Røe & M. Luccarelli, *Green Oslo. Visions. Planning and Discourse.* 230–256. Routledge.

Kjældgaard, L. H. (2018). *Meningen med velfærdsstaten: velfærdsstatsdebat og dansk litteratur 1950-1980.* Gyldendal.

Lecroart, P. & Ming, T. S. (2020). *Oslo. Rebuilding the Highway-City. Hovinbyen & Øtre Aker Vei Projects.* L'Institut Paris Region.

Mattsson, H. & Wallenstein, S.-O. (2010). *Swedish Modernism: Architecture, Consumption, and the Welfare State.* Black Dog Publishing.

Mechlenborg, M. (2019). Reintegrating Ghettos into Society: Lessons Learned from the Danish Ghetto Strategy. *Nordic Journal of Architecture Research, 31*(1), 59–88.

Mouratidis, K. (2022, March). COVID-19 and the compact city: Implications for well-being and sustainable urban planning, *Science of the Total Environment, 811.* https://doi.org/10.1016/j.scitotenv.2021.152332

Nielsen, K. (2009). Fællesskabets posttraditionelle vilkår. In M. Bolt & J. Lund (Eds.), *Fællesskabsfølelser. Kunst, politik, filosofi.* Klim.

Nielsen, T. (2008). *Gode intentioner og uregerlige byer.* Arkitektskolens Forlag.

Næss, P. (2020). Sustainable Development: A Question of 'Modernization' or 'Degrowth'? In A. Hagen & U. Higdem (Eds.), *Innovation in Public Planning.* 91–109. Palgrave Macmillan.

Pedersen, O. K. (2011). *Konkurrencestaten.* Hans Reitzels forlag.

Rasmussen, S. E. (1963). *Tingbjerg: Forklaring til en Byplan.* Steen Eiler Rasmussens Tegnestue.

Regeringen. (2018a). *Ét Danmark uden parallelsamfund. Ingen ghettoer i 2030.* Økonomi- og Indenrigsministeriet.

Regeringen. (2018b). *Nye muligheder for fuld afvikling af de mest udsatte ghettoområder.* Økonomi- og Indenrigsministeriet.

113

Reiermann, J. & Andersen, T. (2019, November 25).
    11.000 mennesker skal finde et andet sted at bo.
    Mandagmorgen.

Reuters. (2021). *Factbox-Dysfunctional Swedish housing marked
    behind ouster of PM Lofven.* https://www.reuters.com/
    article/sweden-housing-idUSL5N2051RM (accessed
    January 31, 2022)

Rogaczewska, N., Lønne, R., & Sørensen, K. F. (2014). *How to
    House.* Danish Social Housing.

Schnell, J. & Skjulhaug, M. (2020). Hyttedebatten handler om
    norsk urbanitet. *Plan* https://plantidsskrift.no/debatt/
    hyttedebatten-handler-om-norsk-urbanitet/ (accessed
    January 31, 2022)

Socialministeriet. (2016). Velfærdspolitisk analyse, *3.* https://
    www.socialministeriet.dk/media/9388/almene-boliger-i-
    danmark.pdf (accessed April 2021)

Stenbro, R., Skorupka, A., Kørte, K. Ø., Lunke, E. B., & Hellvik,
    H. (2016). Suburban Densification in Oslo through the
    Lens of Social and Cultural Sustainability. *Journal of
    Urban Research.* https://doi.org/10.4000/articulo.2958

Svendsen, G. T. (2018). *Trust.* Aarhus University Press.

Swenarton, M., Avermaete, T., & van den Heuvel, D. (Eds.).
    (2014). *Architecture and the Welfare State.* Routledge.

Tan, P. Y. & Rinaldi, B. M. (2019). Landscapes for compact cities.
    Journal of Landscape Architecture, 14(1), 4-7. https://doi:
    10.1080/18626033.2019.1623540

Tietjen, A. (Ed.). (2010). *Forstadens Bygningskultur 1945-1989:
    På sporet af velfærdsforstadens bevaringsværdier.*
    Realdania & Dansk Bygningsarv.

Vejre, H. (2016). Efterkrigstidens planlægning og forvaltning
    af de grønne områder. In C. Christiansen et al. (Eds.),
    *Den Grønne Metropol. Natur og recreative områder i
    hovedstadsmetropolen efter 1900.* 283-344. HOKA.

Vejre, H., Skodborg, L., & Fritzböger, B. (2016). Borgernes skov
    - Vestskovens anlæggelse. In C. Christiansen et al. (Eds.),

Den Grønne Metropol. Natur og recreative områder i hovedstadsmetropolen efter 1900. 393–456. HOKA.

Venter, Z. S., Barton, D.N ., Gundersen, V., Figari, H., & Nowell, M. (2020). Urban nature in a time of crisis: recreational use of green space increases during the COVID-19 outbreak in Oslo, Norway. *Environmental Research Letters*, Lett. 15. https://doi.org/10.1088/1748-9326/abb

Wagenaar, C. (Ed.). (2004). *Happy: Cities and Public Happiness in Post-war Europe*. NAI Publishers.